The Dhammapada

The $\mathcal{D}$HAMMAPADA

धम्मपद

Verses on the Way

A NEW TRANSLATION

of the

TEACHINGS OF THE BUDDHA,

with a

GUIDE TO READING THE TEXT,

by Glenn Wallis

THE MODERN LIBRARY

NEW YORK

Grateful acknowledgment is made to the following for permission to reprint previously published material:

© Bhikkhu Bodhi 1995, 2001. Adapted from *The Middle Length Discourses of the Buddha: A Translation of the Majjhima Nikaya* with permission of Wisdom Publications, 199 Elm Street, Somerville, MA 02144 U.S.A., www.wisdompubs.org

© Maurice Walshe 1987, 1995. Adapted from *The Long Discourses of the Buddha: A Translation of the Digha Nikaya* with permission of Wisdom Publications, 199 Elm Street, Somerville, MA 02144 U.S.A., www.wisdompubs.org

© Bhikkhu Bodhi 1995, 2000. Adapted from *The Connected Discourses of the Buddha: A Translation of the Samyutta Nikaya* with permission of Wisdom Publications, 199 Elm Street, Somerville, MA 02144 U.S.A., www.wisdompubs.org

LIBRARY OF CONGRESS CATALOGING-IN-PUBLICATION DATA
Tipitaka. Suttapitaka. Khuddakanikaya. Dhammapada. English
The Dhammapada : verses on the Way, a new translation of the Teachings of the Buddha, with a guide to reading the text / by Glenn Wallis.
p.   cm.
In English; translated from Pali.
ISBN 0-679-64307-9
1. Spiritual life—Buddhism.   I. Wallis, Glenn.   II. Title.

BQ1372.E64W35 2004
294.3'82322—dc22   2004050464

Modern Library website address: www.modernlibrary.com

Printed in the United States of America on acid-free paper

2 4 6 8 9 7 5 3

This book is dedicated to my father, Robert Wallis,
who gave me the freedom to find my way.

Contents

—ↄ∂ↄ—

GUIDE TO READING THE TEXT

Foreword

———— ✑ ————

Who will master this earth,
this world of death and radiant beings?
Who will gather a well-taught verse on the way,
as a skilled gardener gathers a flower?

For over two thousand years, the *Dhammapada* has been treasured by Buddhists throughout the world for possessing a vibrancy and relevance unlike any other work in the canon. This regard has accorded the text unsurpassed popularity in Buddhist cultures as diverse as ancient Turkistan and modern Thailand, Tibet, and Sri Lanka. Much of the work's popularity is attributable to its accessibility. By distilling the complex models, theories, rhetorical style, and sheer volume of the Buddha's teachings into concise, crystalline verses, the *Dhammapada* makes the Buddhist way of life available to anyone—anyone, that is, who would seek an end to the persistent dissatisfaction known as *dukkha*. In fact, it is possible that the very source of the *Dhammapada* in the third century B.C.E. is traceable to the need of the early Buddhist communities in India to laicize the ascetic impetus of the Buddha's original words. The *Dhammapada* thus serves the dual function of preserving an ancient summation of the copious teachings and giving expression to the universal human concerns animating such an enterprise.

THE TITLE

My translation of the term *dhammapada* as "verses on the way" is intended to bring out these two functions of the work in the history of Buddhism, as well as to reflect my approach to translating the work (which I address in the Guide). The most common rendering of the two terms that make up the title, *dhamma* and *pada,* is apparent in the titles of two modern translations: "path (*pada*) of righteousness (*dhamma*)" or "word (*pada*) of the doctrine (*dhamma*)."*

The first term, *dhamma,* is one of the most multivalent words imaginable in any language. It is derived from the Sanskrit verbal root *dhṛ* (from which comes the better-known form *dharma*), which primarily means "to hold, support, sustain." In Buddhist literature alone its lexical range covers a good deal of ground, for example: phenomena, i.e., elements or things, from an atom to a mountain or a cosmos; mental objects or, roughly, thoughts; any type of quality, personal or physical, abstract or concrete; morality, righteousness; law, foundation, custom, standard; teaching; truth. Add to this the pan-Indian usage of the term as "universal law," and it is not difficult to see why *dhamma* is often translated as "religion."

One way to see how the term functioned is to examine this sentence: The *dhamma* is the *dhamma* because of the *dhamma.* For India's numerous theistic traditions, this means: The religion is the truth because of the universal structure. That is, the religion, being founded on doctrines and practices that conform to universal laws, normatively considered to be of divine origin, is necessarily proper, correct, true. Thus, the religion simultaneously is sustained by the universal law and, in being practiced, serves to sustain natural law further. To Buddhists, most of this statement assumes too much by way of metaphysical presumption—about cosmic origins, divine beings, supernatural forces, foundational laws, dualism of subject and object, a determinative, mind-independent reality, and so on. Nonetheless, the Buddha did claim to have discovered patterns that operate in human life with such regularity and certainty that the term *dhamma* seemed the only appropriate designation for his teachings.

But free from these presuppositions of theistically oriented religions, the term acquires new shades of meaning for Buddhists. Nowhere, the Buddha insisted, were the kinds of powers, forces, and beings that are posited in the narratives of theistic traditions really observable—nowhere, that is, outside the narratives themselves. Thus, the patterns discerned by the Buddha invariably concern *human being* and, hence, *the human being.* For Buddhists, then, the sentence "The *dhamma* is the *dhamma*

---

*David Kalupahana, *A Path of Righteousness* (Lanham: University Press of America, 1986); K. R. Norman, *The Word of the Doctrine (Dhammapada)* (Oxford: Pali Text Society, 1997).

because of the *dhamma*" means something like: "The teaching is the proper way of living because of the way things are." And, unlike in theistic traditions, "the way things are" is, in the Buddhist view, readily observable, here and now, to anyone who would develop the skill to discern it. The *dhamma*, as teaching, is precisely the means to this skill.

The second term, *pada*, also covers a rich variety of meanings. At its root, it denotes three basic actions: "to fall," "to go," and "to participate." Its numerous derivatives include "word," "verse," "foot," "footstep," "path," "trace," and "matter."

Now, how does all of this bear on my translation of *dhammapada* as "verses on the way"? The *Dhammapada* literally asks its reader to turn (*versus*—homonyms are fun!) toward the teaching (*dhamma*), toward the path (*pada*); the verses (*pada*) that compose the work are the seeker's intimate companions on the way (*dhamma*). The "on" here means, of course, both "along" (i.e., while on the journey) and "concerning, about." As a distillation of the Buddha's teachings, the *Dhammapada* constitutes a prescription for proper living, and its sole purpose is to guide the reader along the way that the Buddha saw as the most conducive to that aim.

A Note on the Translation

This book is organized in a way that is meant to encourage a fresh encounter with the *Dhammapada*. The translation, which immediately follows, is given without any explanatory material. It is then followed by the "Guide to Reading the Text." The Guide contains explanatory material in the form of chapter overviews and notes, providing clarification of Buddhist terminology, concepts, and models. Verses discussed in the Guide are marked with asterisks in the translation. I recommend reading through the translation unaided by my comments, and then, on the second, third, fourth, et cetera, reading, referring to the notes as necessary. *A second reading?!* Learning is slow; careful reading is tedious; understanding is elusive. So why not read the *Dhammapada* repeatedly, taking to heart its claim to be a revealer of treasures?

Translation

CHAPTER ONE

Contrasting Pairs

यमकवग्गो

Preceded by mind
are phenomena,
led by mind,
formed by mind.
If with mind polluted
one speaks or acts,
then pain follows,
as a wheel follows
the draft ox's foot.   (1)*

Preceded by mind
are phenomena,
led by mind,
formed by mind.
If with mind pure
one speaks or acts,
then ease follows,
as an ever-present shadow.   (2)*

"He berated me! He hurt me!
He beat me! He deprived me!"
For those who hold such grudges,
hostility is not appeased.   (3)

"He berated me! He hurt me!
He beat me! He deprived me!"
For those who forgo such grudges,
hostility ceases.   (4)

In this world
hostilities are *never*
appeased by hostility.
But by the absence of hostility
are they appeased.
This is an interminable truth.   (5)*

Some do not understand
that we are perishing here.
Those who understand this
bring to rest their quarrels.   (6)

Living with an eye to pleasure,
unrestrained in the sense faculties,
immoderate in eating, indolent, and idle—
Māra overcomes such a person,
as the wind overcomes a weak tree.   (7)*

Living without an eye to pleasure,
well restrained in the sense faculties,
moderate in eating, faithful, and energetic—
Māra does not overcome such a person,
as the wind, a rocky hill.   (8)*

A stained person
who would wear the yellow-stained robe,
although neither honest nor restrained,
is not worthy of the yellow-stained.   (9)*

But a person
who has dispelled his stain,
well set on virtuous ways,

both honest and restrained,
that one is worthy of the yellow-stained.   (10)*

Those who hold the worthless to be of value,
and see in the valuable the worthless,
do not attain the valuable,
pasturing, as they are, in the field of wrong intention.   (11)*

But having understood the valuable as the valuable,
and the worthless as the worthless,
they attain the valuable,
pasturing, as they are, in the field of right intention.   (12)*

Just as rain pierces
a poorly roofed house,
so passion pierces
an uncultivated mind.   (13)*

Just as rain cannot pierce
a well-roofed house,
so passion cannot pierce
a well-cultivated mind.   (14)*

In this world he grieves.
In the world beyond he grieves.
In both worlds, the harm doer grieves.
He grieves, he is struck down by sorrow,
having seen the impurity of his own actions.   (15)*

In this world he rejoices.
In the world beyond he rejoices.
In both worlds, the virtuous person rejoices.
He rejoices, he is uplifted,
having seen the purity of his own actions.   (16)*

In this world he suffers.
In the world beyond he suffers.

In both worlds, the harm doer suffers.
Thinking, "I have acted destructively!" he suffers.
Taking an unfortunate rebirth,
he suffers even more. (17)*

In this world he is delighted.
In the world beyond he is delighted.
In both worlds, the virtuous person is delighted.
Thinking, "I have created value!" he is delighted.
Taking a fortunate rebirth,
he is delighted even more. (18)*

Although reciting many religious texts,
if one does not practice accordingly,
he is a heedless man.
Like a cowherd counting the cows of others,
he has no share in the religious life. (19)*

Although reciting but little from religious texts,
if one is good, he lives in harmony with the teachings.
Abandoning passion, hatred, and delusion,
he possesses proper understanding, perfect purity of mind.
Showing no attachment to this world or beyond,
he has a share in the religious life. (20)*

{*Guide page 103*}

CHAPTER TWO

Diligence

अप्पमादवग्गो

Diligence is the path to the deathless.
Negligence is the path of death.
The diligent do not die.
Those who are negligent
are as the dead.   (21)*

Understanding this distinctly,
those who are skilled in diligence
rejoice in diligence,
delighting in the pasture of the noble ones.   (22)*

Those meditators who persevere,
persistently endeavoring,
are wise ones who touch the unbinding—
that perfect peace from bondage.   (23)*

For the person of energy, thoughtfulness,
pure conduct, considerate action,
restraint, wholesome living, and diligence,
glory increases.   (24)

With energy, diligence,
restraint, and control,

the wise person should make an island
which no flood can overflow. (25)

Childish, unthinking people
indulge negligence.
But the wise person guards diligence
as the greatest treasure. (26)

You should not indulge negligence
or be intimate with sensual delight.
Meditating diligently,
one obtains abundant ease. (27)*

When the skilled person
expels negligence by means of diligence,
he is free from sorrow.
Having ascended the palace of wisdom,
this skilled one gazes down
—as if standing on a mountain—
on the sorrowing people,
the childish ones below
standing on the ground. (28)*

Diligent among the negligent,
ever vigilant among the sleeping,
the wise person moves on
like a swift horse
who has overtaken a weak one. (29)

By means of diligence
Maghavan became
the best of the radiant ones.
Diligence they praise.
Negligence is always censured. (30)*

A practitioner delighting in diligence,
seeing dread in negligence,

advances as a fire—
every fetter, coarse and subtle, burns.   (31)*

A practitioner delighting in diligence,
seeing dread in negligence,
being near to the unbinding
cannot likely fall away.   (32)

{ Guide page 111 }

CHAPTER THREE

Mind

चित्तवग्गो

Trembling and quivering is the mind,
difficult to guard and hard to restrain.
The person of wisdom sets it straight,
as a fletcher does an arrow.

(33)*

Like a fish thrown to the ground,
wrenched from its sheltered home,
this mind trembles,
seized by the sway of death.

(34)*

It is good to tame the mind,
alighting, as it does, wherever it desires—
swift, resistant to restraint.
A tamed mind gives rise to ease.

(35)*

So difficult to perceive, exceedingly subtle,
alighting, as it does, wherever it desires.
Let the person of wisdom guard the mind.
A guarded mind gives rise to ease.

(36)*

Wandering far and alone, intangible,
the mind is hidden in the cave of the body.

Those who would restrain the mind
are liberated from the bonds of Māra.   (37)*

For the one whose mind is unsteady,
who does not know the good way,
whose serenity is wavering,
insightful knowledge is not perfected.   (38)*

There is no fear for the wide awake—
the one who has let go of gain and loss,
whose mind is not moistened by passion,
whose thoughts are unassailed.   (39)*

Considering this body as a pot of clay,
establishing this mind as a fortress,
may you attack Māra with the weapon of wisdom
and, guarding the victory, be free from attachment.   (40)

Soon, for certain,
this body will lie on the ground,
cast away, without consciousness,
like a useless log.   (41)*

Whatever a rival may do to a foe,
or a vengeful person to the one he hates,
a wrongly applied mind would do more
damage to him than that.   (42)

Nothing that a mother, father,
or other relative might do
would do more good for him
than a mind well controlled.   (43)

{ *Guide page 118* }

CHAPTER FOUR

Flowers

पुप्फवग्गो

Who will master this earth,
this world of death and radiant beings?
Who will gather a well-taught verse on the way,
as a skilled gardener gathers a flower? (44)*

A seeker will master this earth,
this world of death and radiant beings.
A seeker will gather a well-taught verse on the way,
as a skilled gardener gathers a flower. (45)*

Considering this body to be as foam,
awakening fully to its nature
as a shimmering mirage,
cutting, like this, the flowers of Māra,
you would walk beyond the sight
of the king of death. (46)*

Death carries away
the person whose mind is engaged
in gathering flowers only,
like a great flood does a sleeping village. (47)

Death seizes
the person whose mind is engaged
in gathering flowers only,
desires yet unsatisfied.

(48)

As a bee flying from a flower,
having taken up its nectar,
does not harm its luster or fragrance,
so should the sage wander in the village.

(49)*

Look not at the faults of others
nor at what they do or leave undone;
but only at your own deeds
and deeds unachieved.

(50)

As a brilliant flower
rich in luster but without scent—
so is a well-spoken word fruitless
for the one who does not act.

(51)

As a brilliant flower
rich in luster and fragrant—
so does a well-spoken word
bear fruit for the one who acts.

(52)

Just as many strands of garlands
may be made from a heap of flowers,
so should a mortal-born person
do much that is beneficial.

(53)

Neither does the fragrance of a flower
nor that of sandalwood or jasmine
flow against the wind.
But the scent of the good
does flow against the wind.
An excellent person diffuses scent
in all directions.

(54)*

Sandalwood, crepe jasmine,
blue lotus, and flowering jasmine—
of the fragrances born of these,
incomparable is the scent of virtue.   (55)

Slight is this fragrance—
jasmine and sandal.
But the scent of a virtuous person
wafts supreme among the radiant ones.   (56)

Māra cannot find the path
to those whose virtue is complete,
living diligently, freed
by perfect understanding.   (57)

As on the road,
in a heap of discarded refuse,
there might be born a lotus
of perfumed fragrance,
pleasing to the mind,   (58)*

so amid those beings,
common and blind,
who have become as refuse,
a disciple of the fully awakened one,
by means of insightful knowledge, shines.   (59)*

{ *Guide page 121* }

CHAPTER FIVE

The Childish Person
बालवग्गो

The night is long for the wide awake.
The mile is long for the weary.
The round of birth and death is long
for childish people, who do not know the good way.   (60)*

If you cannot find a companion
who is better than or like yourself,
you should make your way, steadily, alone.
In the childish there is no companionship.   (61)

Thinking, "I have children and wealth!"
—the childish person becomes anxious.
For oneself there is not even a self.
Whence then sons and wealth?   (62)*

A childish person considering his folly
is thereby even as a skilled one.
But a childish person considering himself skilled
is rightly called "childish."   (63)

Even if throughout his life
a childish one attends the skilled,

he does not thereby discern the way,
as the spoon, the taste of soup.

(64)

Even if for just an instant
an intelligent person attends the skilled,
he quickly discerns the way,
as the tongue, the taste of soup.

(65)

Childish, unthinking people
go through life as enemies to themselves,
committing detrimental actions
that bear bitter fruit.

(66)*

That act is not beneficial which,
having been committed, one regrets,
the fruit of which one receives
crying, face full of tears.

(67)*

But that act is beneficial which,
having been committed, one does not regret,
the fruit of which one receives
pleased and content.

(68)*

As long as the damage has not borne fruit,
the childish one considers it as honey.
But when the damage bears fruit,
then the childish one suffers affliction.

(69)

Month after month the childish person
might eat his meal with a blade of grass;
yet he would still not be worth a fraction
of those who have discerned the way.

(70)*

Like milk, a detrimental action, once committed,
does not at once congeal.
Smoldering, it follows the childish person
like a fire concealed in ashes.

(71)

To his misfortune only
is knowledge born for the childish person:
it strikes his good fortune,
causing it to descend on his head. (72)

He would desire unwarranted prestige,
preeminence among practitioners,
authority over their dwellings,
and to be honored by families
other than his own. (73)

"Let both the householder and the wanderer
think that this was done by me alone;
let them be dependent on me for all of their duties."
This is the intention of the childish person,
so desire and pride increase. (74)*

There is one way for acquiring things,
another leading to the unbinding.
Knowing this, the practitioner,
the disciple of the Buddha,
should not take pleasure in honor—
let him foster detachment. (75)*

{*Guide page 125*}

CHAPTER SIX

The Skilled Person

पण्डितवग्गो

Regard the person who sees your faults
as a revealer of treasures.
Associate with that skilled person
as one who is wise, who speaks reprovingly.
Keeping company with such a person,
things get better, not worse.   (76)*

He should exhort, instruct,
and restrain you from poor behavior.
To the good he is endearing,
to the bad he is unpleasant.   (77)*

He would not associate with harmful friends.
He would not associate with the lowest of people.
So, you should associate with encouraging friends;
you should associate with the best of people.   (78)*

He who imbibes the teaching
rests happily, with a clear mind.
The skilled person delights always
in the way revealed by the noble ones.   (79)*

Irrigators guide the water.
Fletchers shape the arrow shaft.

Carpenters shape wood.
The skilled tame themselves. (80)

As a rock of single solid mass
cannot be moved by the wind,
so are the skilled unshaken
by praise and blame. (81)

As a deep pond, clear, calm,
so do the skilled become serene,
having heard the teachings. (82)

Good people stand apart everywhere.
The good do not initiate conversation
out of desire for enjoyment.
Touched now by pleasure, now by pain,
the skilled do not expose their highs and lows. (83)

Neither for your own nor for another's sake
should you wish for a son, wealth, or empire.
You should not wish for your own success
if acquired by improper means.
You should be virtuous, wise, and honorable. (84)

Few are those among the people
who cross to the other shore.
The rest of humanity just runs about
on the bank right here before us. (85)*

But those people who follow the way
when the teaching is well proclaimed
will go to the other shore.
The realm of death is so hard to traverse. (86)*

Having left the dark way,
the skilled person should cultivate the bright.
Coming from his home to no home,
in seclusion, where enjoyment is hard to find, (87)*

there he should hope for delight.
Having forsaken all desires, possessing nothing,
the skilled person should cleanse himself
of the afflictions of his mind.   (88)*

Those whose minds are well trained
in the factors of full awakening
who delight, without clinging,
in the renunciation of grasping—
such bright ones, impulses destroyed,
are, in this very world, unbound.   (89)*

{ Guide page 131 }

CHAPTER SEVEN

The Accomplished Person

अरहन्तवग्गो

There is no fever for the person
who has completed the journey—
free from sorrow,
freed in every respect,
the knots removed. (90)*

The mindful strive.
They do not delight in shelter.
Like cranes quitting the moor,
they forsake home after home. (91)*

Those for whom there is no amassing,
who understand fully the nature of food,
free, empty, and without conditions
is their sphere of action.
As birds in space, their way is hard to trace. (92)*

His impulses exhausted
and nutriments starved,
free, empty, and without conditions
is his sphere of action.
As birds in space, his way is hard to trace. (93)*

His senses serene
like horses well tamed by the charioteer,
the person who has let go of haughtiness,
who is free from impulses—
even the radiant ones are envious of one such as that. (94)

Like the earth, he is not troubled.
Like a pillar he is firm.
Like a pond free from mud
there are no rounds of rebirths
for such a person. (95)

Calmed is the mind,
calmed, speech and action
of one set free by genuine knowledge.
For such a person
there is peace. (96)

The person who is beyond faith
and understands the unconditioned,
who cuts off rebirth, forgoes opportunity,
and gives up wishing—
that one is a superior person. (97)*

Whether in a village or in the forest,
whether in a valley or on high ground,
delightful is the place
where accomplished ones dwell. (98)

Delightful are the forests
where no worldly person takes delight.
Those who are free from passion will delight there;
those who seek sensual pleasure will not. (99)

{ *Guide page 135* }

CHAPTER EIGHT

Thousands

सहस्सवग्गो

Better than a thousand statements
composed of meaningless words
is a single meaningful word which,
having been heard, brings peace.   (100)

Better than a thousand verses
composed of meaningless words
is a single word of verse which,
having been heard, brings peace.   (101)

And if one should recite a hundred verses
composed of meaningless words,
better is a single verse on the way which,
having been heard, brings peace.   (102)

Though one might conquer in battle
a thousand times a thousand men,
the one who conquers himself alone
is supreme in battle.   (103)

It is better indeed to conquer yourself
rather than other people.

For a person who tames himself
acting consciously always,   (104)

neither a radiant one nor an aerial spirit,
nor Māra together with Brahmā
could turn into defeat the victory
of a person such as that.   (105)

Month after month one might offer
a thousand sacrifices for a hundred years.
And another might, for an instant only,
honor a person who cultivates himself.
Better is that honoring than the one
which was offered for a hundred years.   (106)

A person might worship fire
in the forest for a hundred years.
And another might, for an instant only,
honor a person who cultivates himself.
Better is that honoring than the one
which was offered for a hundred years.   (107)

Whatever sacrifice and offering in this world
a person who is intent on value might sacrifice for a year,
even that in its entirety does not amount to a fraction.
Better is it to respect those who live honestly.   (108)

For the person of respectful character
who always honors his elders,
these four qualities increase:
life span, appearance, happiness, and strength.   (109)

Better than living a hundred years
poor in virtue, unfocused,
is a single day lived
as a virtuous meditator.   (110)

Better than living a hundred years
poor in understanding, unfocused,
is a single day lived
as an insightful meditator.

(111)

Better than living a hundred years
lethargic, low in energy,
is a single day lived
exerting steadfast vigor.

(112)

Better than living a hundred years
not seeing arising and passing away,
is a single day lived
arising and passing away seen.

(113)

Better than living a hundred years
not seeing the path to the deathless,
is a single day lived as one who sees
the path to the deathless.

(114)

Better than living a hundred years
not seeing the supreme way,
is a single day lived as one who sees
the supreme way.

(115)

{*Guide page 138*}

CHAPTER NINE

Detriment

पापवग्गो

In goodness be quick!
Restrain your thought from detriment.
For a person who creates value slowly,
the mind delights in detriment. (116)*

If a person does something detrimental,
he should not do it again and again.
He must not create that impulse in himself.
Pain is the accumulation of detriment. (117)

If a person does something valuable,
he should do it again and again.
He must create that impulse in himself.
Ease is the accumulation of value. (118)

Even a person who acts to his
own detriment has good fortune
as long as his misdeed has not matured.
But when the misdeed has matured
then that person experiences misfortunes. (119)

Even a good person experiences injury
as long as his goodness has not matured.
But when the good has matured
then the good person experiences benefit. (120)

One should not think slightly of injury—
"that will not come to *me*."
With drops of falling water
even a water pot is filled.
The childish person is full of injury
gathered day by day. (121)

One should not think slightly of value—
"that will not come to *me*."
With drops of falling water
even a water pot is filled.
The wise person is full of value
gathered day by day. (122)

Detrimental action is to be avoided
as a lonely merchant with great riches
would avoid a dangerous road
or as one who desires life, poison. (123)

If there were no wound on the hand,
poison could be handled with that hand.
Poison does not penetrate where there is no wound.
There is no detriment for one who does not commit it. (124)

Whoever wrongs a person of slight culpability,
a person who is pure and free from flaws,
injury falls back on that childish one
like fine dust cast against the wind. (125)

Many are born in a womb,
those who act destructively, in the lower world;
those of good conduct go to a higher world,
those who are without impulses, to perfect unbinding. (126)*

Not in the sky,
not in the depths of the sea,
not by entering a cleft in the mountains,
nowhere in the world can there be found
a place where one might be released
from detrimental actions. (127)

Not in the sky,
not in the depths of the sea,
not by entering a cleft in the mountains,
nowhere in the world can there be found
a place where death would not prevail. (128)

{ *Guide page 139* }

CHAPTER TEN

Violence

दण्डवग्गो

All tremble before violence.
All fear death.
Having done the same yourself,
you should neither harm nor kill. (129)

All tremble before violence.
Life is held dear by all.
Having done the same yourself,
you should neither harm nor kill. (130)

Whoever, through violence, does harm
to living beings desiring ease,
hoping for such ease himself,
will not, when he dies, realize ease. (131)

Whoever does no harm through violence
to living beings desiring ease,
hoping for such ease himself,
will, when he dies, realize ease. (132)

Do not speak harshly to anyone.
Those to whom you speak
might respond to you.

Angry talk really is painful.
The result might crash down on you. (133)

If, like a piece of metal when struck,
you yourself do not resound,
can it be that you have achieved unbinding
—there is no anger found in you? (134)

Like a cowherd driving cattle
to pasture with a staff,
so aging and death
drive human life. (135)

But a childish person does not realize
that he is performing detrimental actions.
The unthinking one is tormented
by his own actions,
like one burned by fire. (136)*

Whoever harms with violence
those who are gentle and innocent,
to one of these ten states
that person quickly descends: (137)

he would beget
severe suffering;
deprivation and fracturing
of the body; or grave illness, too;
mental imbalance; (138)

trouble from the government;
cruel slander;
loss of relatives;
or destruction of property. (139)

Or a raging fire burns his dwellings.
After the dissolution of his body
the unwise one falls into the lower world. (140)

Neither naked wandering
nor matted hair, nor mud,
fasting, lying on the ground;
neither dust nor dirt,
nor austere crouching,
can purify a person
who has not overcome doubt.   (141)*

If, even though an adorned layman,
a person practices equanimity, is tranquil,
mild, restrained, living the lofty life,
he, having lain down violence
toward all sentient beings,
is a superior person, a seeker, a practitioner.   (142)*

Is a conscientious person
found anywhere in this world,
one who responds even slightly to reproach,
as a good horse responds to the whip?   (143)

Like a good horse
sensitive to the whip,
be ardent and quickened.
By means of faith, morality, effort,
meditative concentration, investigation of the teaching,
perfect knowledge and conduct, and mindfulness,
you will abandon this substantial mass of pain.   (144)*

Irrigators guide the water.
Fletchers shape the arrow shaft.
Carpenters shape wood.
The virtuous tame themselves.   (145)

{ *Guide page 142* }

CHAPTER ELEVEN

Old Age

जरावग्गो

What laughter is there, what joy,
when all is perpetually ablaze?
Enfolded in darkness,
do you not seek a lamp?   (146)*

Look at this beautified image
composed of wounds amassed.
Full of sickness, yet desired by many,
it has neither permanence nor constancy.   (147)

Worn out is this body,
a frail nest of disease.
This festering mass breaks apart,
for life has death as its end.   (148)

Like gourds
cast off in autumn
are these gray bones.
Seeing them as such—what joy?   (149)

A fortress built of bones
plastered with blood and skin,
wherein are hidden
death and decay,
pride and pretense.   (150)

Even the colorful chariots of kings age.
The body, too, grows old.
But the way of those who are good
does not grow old,
for the good teach it
to those of fine character.   (151)

An uninstructed person
ages like an ox:
his bulk increases,
his insight does not.   (152)

I have coursed through the whirl
of numerous lives
seeking, but not finding,
the builder of the house.
Pain is birth over and over again.   (153)*

Builder of the house—you are seen!
Never again will you build a house.
These rafters all broken,
the roof of the house destroyed,
the mind, free from the conditioned,
has come to the end of cravings.   (154)*

The lofty life unlived,
the treasure in youth unattained,
people dry up like aged herons
in a lake without fish.   (155)

The lofty life unlived,
the treasure in youth unattained,
people lie like broken arrows,
lamenting the past.   (156)

CHAPTER TWELVE

Oneself
अत्तवग्गो

If you hold yourself dear
you should guard yourself well.
A skilled person would
take care of himself
throughout the three
watches of the night. (157)

First, he should establish himself
in what is proper.
Then, he should instruct another.
The skilled person would thus not suffer. (158)

If he himself would act
as he instructs another,
then, well restrained,
he should train others.
It is oneself, as they say,
that is so hard to restrain. (159)

You are master of yourself.
What other master could there be?

It is by restraining oneself
that one attains the master—
so difficult to attain. (160)

The damage done by oneself,
born of oneself, arising from oneself,
grinds the unthinking person
like a diamond grinds a jewel made of stone. (161)

The person whose
extremely poor comportment
is spread out like a vine on a tree
acts toward himself
as his enemy would wish. (162)

It is easy to do things
that are destructive
or harmful to oneself.
The beneficial and productive—
that is very difficult to do. (163)

The person who scorns
the teaching of the accomplished ones,
of the noble ones living the way,
is an unthinking person,
pursuing a harmful view.
Like the fruits of a reed,
he ripens toward his own destruction. (164)

By oneself is damage done:
by oneself is one defiled.
By oneself is damage not done:
by oneself is one purified.
Purity and impurity come from oneself.
No one can purify another. (165)

One should not neglect one's goal
for the goal of another, even if great.

Knowing well his goal,
let him be a person who pursues
the true goal.   (166)

{*Guide page 147*}

CHAPTER THIRTEEN

The World

लोकवग्गो

Do not embrace an inferior way,
or live a life of negligence.
Do not embrace a wrong view,
or be a person who indulges in this world. (167)

Arise! Do not be neglectful.
Practice the teaching well.
The person who practices the teaching
dwells in ease in this world and beyond. (168)

Practice the teaching well.
The teaching should not be poorly practiced.
The person who practices the teaching
dwells in ease in this world and beyond. (169)

As one would look upon a bubble
or gaze at a mirage—
watching the world like this,
you are not seen by the king of death. (170)*

Come, look at this world.
It is like a king's colorful chariot
where childish people settle in.
For those who know,
there is no attraction.   (171)*

But the person who,
having once been neglectful,
is no longer neglectful
brightens this world
like the moon freed from a cloud.   (172)

The person whose
detrimental action, though done,
is obstructed by a skillful one,
brightens this world
like the moon freed from a cloud.   (173)

Darkened is this world.
Few have insight here.
Like a bird set free from a net,
few go to a higher world.   (174)

Swans follow the path of the sun,
moving in space by means of their power.
The wise are guided away from the world,
having conquered Māra and his army.   (175)

There is no damage that cannot be done
by a person who has neglected this single matter—
who engages in false speech
and has rejected the world beyond.   (176)*

Selfish people do not go to the world of the radiant ones.
Childish people do not commend giving.
But the wise person, rejoicing in giving,
is thereby at ease in the world beyond.   (177)

Better than sole sovereignty
over the earth, going to a higher world,
or dominion over the cosmos
is the fruit of entering the stream.   (178)*

{ *Guide page 149* }

CHAPTER FOURTEEN

The Awakened

बुद्धवग्गो

The person whose victory is not diminished,
whose victory no one in the world can touch,
that one is awakened, of limitless sphere, trackless.
By what path would you lead that one?   (179)*

The person for whom there is
no ensnaring, entangling craving
to lead him anywhere at all,
that one is awakened, of limitless sphere, trackless.
By what path would you lead that one?   (180)

They are wise who pursue meditation,
delighting in the calm of renunciation.
Even the radiant ones long for those
who are fully awakened, the mindful.   (181)

Difficult is the attainment of a human birth.
Difficult is the life of mortals.
Difficult is the hearing of the good way.
Difficult is the appearance of those who have awakened.   (182)*

The refraining from all that is harmful,
the undertaking of what is skillful,

the cleansing of one's mind—
this is the teaching of the awakened.   (183)*

Enduring patience is the highest austerity.
The awakened ones say that unbinding is supreme.
A person who injures has certainly not begun to practice;
one who harms others is not a seeker.   (184)

Not abusing, not harming,
restraint in line with the discipline,
moderation in eating and seclusion in dwelling,
exertion in meditation as well—
this is the teaching of the awakened.   (185)

Not through a torrent of money
or in sensual enjoyment
can satisfaction be found.
The skilled person, knowing that
sensual enjoyment is painful,
yielding but little pleasure,   (186)

does not take delight
even in divine enjoyments.
A person who delights
in the dissolution of craving
is a disciple of the perfectly awakened.   (187)

People who are anxious with fear
often go for refuge to mountains and forests,
to tree shrines in pleasant groves.   (188)

This is not a secure refuge.
This is not the best refuge.
Arriving at that refuge,
a person is not released from all pain.   (189)*

But whoever has gone for refuge
to the Buddha, Dhamma, and Saṅgha,

sees with thorough understanding
the four noble truths: (190)*

pain, the arising of pain,
the overcoming of pain,
and the noble eightfold path
leading to the stilling of pain.   (191)*

This is the secure refuge.
This is the best refuge.
Arriving at this refuge,
a person is released from all pain.   (192)

An excellent person is rare;
one is not born just anywhere.
Wherever that wise one is born
the family abounds in happiness.   (193)

Happy is the appearance of awakened ones.
Happy is the teaching of the good way.
Happy is the concord of the community.
Happy is the persistent practice of those in harmony.   (194)

For one who honors those worthy of honor,
whether awakened ones or disciples,
those who have completely overcome
obsessive activity and complexity
and crossed over from lamentation and grief;   (195)*

for one who honors such as those,
those who are at peace, having nothing to fear,
the value earned cannot be fathomed by anyone
as being just so much.   (196)

{ *Guide page 152* }

CHAPTER FIFTEEN

Being at Ease

सुखवग्गो

Oh, with what ease we live
when peaceful amid the hostile!
Amid hostile people
we live peacefully. (197)*

Oh, with what ease we live
when well amid the afflicted!
Amid afflicted people
we live in wellness. (198)

Oh, with what ease we live
when relaxed amid the anxious!
Amid anxious people
we live relaxed. (199)

Oh, with what ease we live,
we who have nothing!
We will become as the radiant ones,
feeding on joy! (200)

Victory begets hostility:
the defeated person lives ill at ease.

Giving up both victory and defeat,
the peaceful person lives at ease. (201)*

There is no fire like passion.
There is no fault like hatred.
There is no pain like the aggregates.
There is no ease surpassing peace. (202)*

Appetite is the most serious disease.
Fabrications are the severest lack of ease.
Knowing this just as it is—
unbinding, the supreme ease. (203)*

Health is the finest possession.
Contentment is the ultimate wealth.
Trustworthy people are the best relatives.
Unbinding is the supreme ease. (204)

Having drunk the sap of solitude
and the savor of peace,
one is free of distress,
free from wrongdoing,
enjoying the delightful
flavor of the teaching. (205)

It is beneficial to see noble people.
In their company one is always at ease.
Not seeing childish people,
one would live in perpetual ease. (206)

The person who associates with the childish
suffers for a long time.
Keeping company with the childish,
like being constantly with an enemy, is painful.
But a wise person is one who dwells in ease,
like a gathering of relatives. (207)

Firm, insightful, knowledgeable,
fastened to morality, devout, noble—
you should follow a person like this,
a good person possessing real wisdom,
like the moon follows the path of the stars. (208)

{ Guide page 159 }

CHAPTER SIXTEEN

Pleasing

पियवग्गो

Engaging himself in what is unfit
and not engaging in what is fitting,
having abandoned the goal,
the person who grasps after what is pleasing
envies the person who applies himself. (209)

Do not be attached to what is pleasing,
and never to that which is unpleasing.
Not seeing what is pleasing is painful,
as is seeing the unpleasing. (210)

For this reason, you should not make things pleasing;
for the absence of what is pleasing is troubling.
There are no bonds for those people
for whom there is no notion of pleasing and unpleasing. (211)

Sorrow springs from what is pleasing.
Fear springs from what is pleasing.
For the person freed from what is pleasing
there is no sorrow. From where could fear emerge? (212)*

Sorrow springs from liking.
Fear springs from liking.
For the person freed from liking
there is no sorrow. From where could fear emerge? (213)

Sorrow springs from attachment.
Fear springs from attachment.
For the person freed from attachment
there is no sorrow. From where could fear emerge? (214)

Sorrow springs from sensual pleasure.
Fear springs from sensual pleasure.
For the person freed from sensual pleasure
there is no sorrow. From where could fear emerge? (215)

Sorrow springs from craving.
Fear springs from craving.
For the person freed from craving
there is no sorrow. From where could fear emerge? (216)

People hold dear the person
who is endowed with virtue and vision,
established in the teaching,
truthful in speech,
and who does the work that is his. (217)

The person who would bring forth
a desire for the nameless, mind clear,
thought not enmeshed in sensual pleasures,
is called "one who is streaming upward." (218)*

Long absent, a person returns safely from afar.
Relatives, friends, and companions
joyously greet the one who has returned. (219)

In the same way, just deserts receive
the person who has created value
and passed from this world to the world beyond,
as relatives receive a loved one who has returned. (220)

{ *Guide page 161* }

CHAPTER SEVENTEEN

Anger

कोघवग्गो

One should abandon anger.
One should give up pride.
One should throw off every fetter.
Troubles do not befall the person
who, possessing nothing,
does not cling to body and mind.   (221)*

The person who can restrain
anger that has arisen
like a reckless chariot—
that one I call a driver.
Other people just hold on to the reins.   (222)

Win over an angry person with poise.
Win over a mean one with kindness.
Win over a greedy person with generosity,
and one who speaks falsely with honesty.   (223)*

One should speak truthfully;
one should not get angry;
when asked, one should give,

even if there is just a little.
With these three traits,
one would go in the presence
of the radiant ones. (224)

Those gentle sages,
constantly restrained in body,
go to that unshakable place where,
having gone, they do not suffer. (225)*

For those who are always watchful,
learning day and night,
intent on unbinding,
the impulses come to rest. (226)

Atula, this is from long ago, it is not recent:
they find fault with one who sits silently,
they find fault with one who speaks much,
they find fault with one who speaks but little.
There is no one in this world who is not faulted. (227)*

There was not, nor will there be,
and now at present no person is found
who is wholly praised or wholly faulted. (228)

But the wise, observing him carefully day after day,
praise that person who is faultless in conduct,
intelligent, and well composed in wisdom and virtue. (229)

Like pure gold,
who is able to find fault with that one?
The radiant ones praise him.
By Brahma, too, he is praised. (230)

Guard against bodily agitation.
Be restrained in the body.
Abandoning bodily misconduct,
act properly with the body. (231)*

Guard against verbal agitation.
Be restrained in speech.
Abandoning verbal misconduct,
act properly with speech.   (232)*

Guard against mental agitation.
Be restrained in the mind.
Abandoning mental misconduct,
act properly with the mind.   (233)*

Those wise ones, restrained in the body,
restrained as well in speech,
those wise ones, restrained in the mind,
they indeed are perfectly restrained.   (234)

{Guide page 163}

CHAPTER EIGHTEEN

Toxins

मलवग्गो

You are now as a withered leaf.
Even the dead have appeared to you.
You stand in the face of death,
yet have no provisions for the journey.   (235)

Fashion a lamp for yourself!
Strive quickly! Become skilled!
Toxins cleansed, free from taints,
you will go to the divine realm
of the noble ones.   (236)*

You are now advanced in age.
You are proceeding toward the presence of death;
and there is no dwelling place for you on the way.
Yet you have no provisions for the journey.   (237)

Fashion a lamp for yourself!
Strive quickly! Become skilled!
Toxins cleansed, free from stain,
you will no longer undergo birth and old age.   (238)

Gradually, little by little, moment by moment,
the wise person should flush toxins from himself,
as a metalsmith cleanses dross from silver.   (239)

As rust emerging from iron
corrodes that very thing from which it emerges,
so the actions of a person who overindulges
lead to an unfortunate rebirth. (240)

The rust of religious texts is nonrepetition.
The rust of houses is lack of repair.
Lethargy is the rust of personal appearance.
Negligence is the rust of the watchman. (241)

The toxin of a woman is misconduct.
Stinginess is the toxin of a giver.
Destructive qualities are toxic in this world and beyond. (242)

More toxic than rust
is ignorance, the greatest toxin.
Eliminating this toxin,
be flawless, you practitioners! (243)

It is easy to live a life
without scruples or shame,
boldly and offensively,
boastfully, recklessly, corruptly. (244)

But it is difficult to live
as a person with scruples,
longing always for purity,
with a simple lifestyle,
open, careful, and perceptive. (245)

Whoever destroys life in the world
or speaks wrongly,
takes what was not given,
or goes to another's wife, (246)

or a person who
drinks intoxicating liquors,

digs up his own root
in this very world. (247)

Know this, friend:
destructive qualities are unimpeded.
Do not let greed and immorality
subject you to pain for long. (248)

People give according to their faith,
according to their kindness.
The person who becomes upset
about others' food and drink,
does not attain, by day or night,
meditative concentration. (249)

But by the person in whom this is cut off,
destroyed at the root, removed,
meditative concentration is attained
by day or by night. (250)

There is no fire like passion.
There is no seizure like hatred.
There is no snare like delusion.
There is no river like craving. (251)

It is easy to see the faults of others,
but difficult to see one's own.
The faults of others you sift like a husk,
but conceal your own, like a deceitful gambler
conceals a bad roll of the die. (252)

For the person who observes the faults of others,
always gazing and critical, the impulses increase.
That person is far from the dissolution of the impulses. (253)

There is no path in space.
There is no seeking externally.
The people delight in

obsessive activity and complexity.
From these, Buddhas are free.   (254)*

There is no path in space.
There is no seeking externally.
Fabrications are not eternal.
There is no agitation in awakened ones.   (255)

{Guide page 166}

CHAPTER NINETEEN

Firmly on the Way

धम्मट्ठवग्गो

A person is not firmly on the way
who would rashly settle a matter.
But one who can distinguish between
both what is and what is not the matter,
a skilled person,   (256)

leads others carefully, ethically, impartially.
Protected by the teaching, intelligent—
that one is called "one who is firmly on the way."   (257)

A person is not skilled
just because he talks a lot.
Peaceful, friendly, secure—
that one is called "skilled."   (258)

A person is not an expert on the teaching
just because he talks a lot.
But the one who, learning but little,
observes the teaching with his body—
one who is not negligent of the teaching—
that person is an expert on the teaching.   (259)*

A person is not venerable
just because his head has gray hair.
His age ripened, he is called
"one who has grown old in vain."   (260)*

But a person in whom there is
truthfulness, morality, gentleness,
restraint, and self-control—
that person, toxins dispelled, wise,
is called "venerable."   (261)

Neither by means of speech alone
nor physical beauty does a person who is
envious, crafty, and greedy
become respectable.   (262)

But the person for whom these are cut off,
destroyed at the root, abolished,
that person, hatred dispelled, wise,
is called "respectable."   (263)

Not by means of a shaven head
does a person who acts unethically
and speaks falsely become a seeker.
How does a person who is full of
longing and greed become a seeker?   (264)

But whoever stills negativity,
coarse or subtle, in every way,
because of the stilling of that negativity,
that person is called a "seeker."   (265)*

A person is not a monk
just because he begs others.
For the very reason that a person
conforms to a domestic way of life
he is not a monk.   (266)*

But a person who has put aside
gain and loss here,
who lives the lofty life
coursing carefully in the world,
that one is called a "monk."   (267)

It is not by means of silence
that an ignorant, foolish person
becomes a sage.
But a skilled person who,
as if holding up a scale,
puts in what is valuable   (268)*

and rejects what is detrimental is a sage.
It is for this reason that he is a sage.
He who gauges these two in the world
is thereby called a "sage."   (269)

A person who harms living beings is not noble.
By being gentle to all living beings
one is called "noble."   (270)*

Not by mere morality,
nor by much learning,
nor through the attainment
of meditative concentration,
nor by solitary living,   (271)

can I touch the ease of renunciation,
not practiced by the ordinary person.
O practitioner, do not be content until
the impulses have been dissolved!   (272)

{*Guide page 170*}

CHAPTER TWENTY

The Path

मग्गवग्गो

Of paths, the best is the eightfold;
of truths, the four statements.
Dispassion is the best of qualities,
and of humans, the one with eyes to see.   (273)*

This is the path, there is no other
for the purification of vision.
Follow this one;
this is confusing to Māra.   (274)

Following this one,
you will bring pain to an end.
This path was proclaimed by me,
after realizing the way to remove the sting.   (275)

It is up to you to strive ardently.
The Buddhas are those
who make known the way.
Those who follow, practicing meditation,
are released from Māra's bond.   (276)

When through insight a person sees
all fabrications are impermanent,
then in pain he turns away.
This is the path to purification. (277)*

When through insight a person sees
all fabrications are painful,
then in pain he turns away.
This is the path to purification. (278)

When through insight a person sees
all fabrications are nonsubstantial,
then in pain he turns away.
This is the path to purification. (279)

A person who is listless
when it is time for exertion,
who is young and strong,
though filled with torpor,
mind possessed of depressing thoughts,
inactive, lethargic, does not
find the path to insightful knowledge. (280)

Watchful of your speech,
in mind and body well restrained,
you should not act unskillfully.
Cleanse these three pathways of action.
Fulfill the path that was revealed by the seers. (281)*

From practice springs
expansive understanding;
from lack of practice, its loss.
Being aware of this divided pathway
to cultivation and decline,
conduct yourself so that understanding increases. (282)

Cut down the forest of desire, not the tree.
From the forest of desire arises fear.

Cutting down both the forest of desire
and the underbrush of lust,
be without craving-forests, practitioners!   (283)*

For, as long as the underbrush of lust
is not cut away—
even a subtle desire
of a man for women—
so long is his mind bound up,
like a suckling calf to its mother.   (284)

Tear out your self-regard
as you would an autumn lily with your hand.
Foster only the path to peace, to unbinding,
taught by the one who traveled it well.   (285)

I will dwell here during the rains,
here in the summer and winter—
so thinks the childish person,
unaware of the obstacles.   (286)

As a great flood carries off a sleeping village,
death carries off the person
whose mind is distracted,
intoxicated by possessions and children.   (287)*

Children cannot provide a shelter,
nor can a father or even a family,
for a person seized by death.
There is no shelter in relatives.   (288)

So, aware of this convincing reason,
the skilled person, restrained by integrity,
should quickly clear the path
leading to the unbinding.   (289)

{ *Guide page 173* }

CHAPTER TWENTY-ONE

Scattered Themes

पकिण्णवग्गो

If by forgoing modest ease
he would see abundant ease,
the wise person, realizing abundant ease,
should forgo modest ease. (290)

The person who wishes ease for himself
through causing pain to others,
contaminated by contact with hostility,
he is not released from hostility. (291)

What should be done, that is neglected;
what should not be done, that is performed.
For those who are haughty and negligent,
the impulses increase. (292)

But those who have fully undertaken
continual mindfulness regarding the body,
persevering in what should be done,
do not do what should not be done.
For those who are mindful, attentive,
the impulses come to rest. (293)

Having killed mother, father,
and two warrior kings,
having destroyed a kingdom
together with its retinue,
the Brahmin goes undisturbed.   (294)*

Having killed mother, father,
and two learned kings,
having killed a tiger as the fifth,
the Brahmin goes undisturbed.   (295)*

The disciples of Gotama
always rise to perfect awakening.
For them, day and night, there is
continual mindfulness of the Buddha.   (296)*

The disciples of Gotama
always rise to perfect awakening.
For them, day and night, there is
continual mindfulness of the teaching.   (297)

The disciples of Gotama
always rise to perfect awakening.
For them, day and night, there is
continual mindfulness of the community.   (298)

The disciples of Gotama
always rise to perfect awakening.
For them, day and night, there is
continual mindfulness of the body.   (299)

The disciples of Gotama
always rise to perfect awakening.
For them, day and night,
the mind delights in gentleness.   (300)

The disciples of Gotama
always rise to perfect awakening.

For them, day and night,
the mind delights in meditation. (301)

It is difficult to leave worldly life,
it is difficult to delight in that.
It is hard to live at home,
the home life is painful.
It is painful to live with discordant people.
The traveler is afflicted with pain.
So, do not be a traveler.
Do not be afflicted with pain. (302)

The faithful person, endowed with virtue,
possessing wealth and fame,
to whatever place he resorts,
there he is honored. (303)

Good people illumine from afar,
like the snowy Himalaya.
Those who are not good
are unperceived here,
like arrows shot in the night. (304)

Sitting alone, resting alone,
wandering alone, unwearied.
Alone, taming himself,
he would be delighted in the forest. (305)

{Guide page 176}

CHAPTER TWENTY-TWO

The Lower World

निरयवग्गो

The person who claims
what is not the case
goes to the lower world,
as does the one who, having acted,
says, "I did not do it."
They both become the same after death:
people of degrading actions in the world beyond. (306)

Many who wear the yellow around their necks
possess destructive qualities, lacking restraint.
These destructive ones, by means of destructive actions,
are reborn in the lower world. (307)*

It is better that a person
eat an iron ball, glowing like a flame,
than the alms food of an entire country,
if that person is poor in virtue and lacking restraint. (308)

A negligent person
who pursues another's wife
encounters four conditions:
a loss of self-worth, disturbed sleep,

disgrace as the third,
the lower world as the fourth.   (309)

A loss of self-worth, a detrimental rebirth,
petty pleasure of a frightened man and woman,
and the government applies a harsh punishment:
so, a person should not embrace another's wife.   (310)

As grass that is hard to grasp
cuts the hand itself,
the seeker's life mishandled
pulls one down to the lower world.   (311)

For any inattentive act,
for an inconsistent practice,
or a dubious religious life
there is no abundant fruit.   (312)

If something is to be done,
one should proceed firmly.
The inattentive practitioner
is more scattered than the dust.   (313)

A destructive act is better undone,
for it consumes one with regret afterwards.
But a constructive act,
doing which one does not regret,
is better done.   (314)

Like a border city
that is protected inside and out,
you should protect yourselves.
Do not let the moment pass by;
for those who miss the moment
grieve, consigned to the lower world.   (315)

Ashamed of what is not shameful,
not ashamed of what is shameful—

because people hold on to false views
they go to an unfortunate rebirth. (316)

Perceiving fear in what is not fearful,
not perceiving fear in what is fearful—
because people hold on to false views
they go to an unfortunate rebirth. (317)

Thinking that there is fault
where there is no fault,
not seeing fault where there is fault—
because people hold on to false views
they go to an unfortunate rebirth. (318)

But knowing a fault as a fault,
and lack of fault as lack of fault,
because people hold on to correct views
they go to a fortunate rebirth. (319)

{ Guide page 178 }

CHAPTER TWENTY-THREE

Elephant

नागवग्गो

As an elephant in battle
bears the arrow shot from a bow,
I will endure insult;
for many people have poor self-control. (320)

They lead a tamed elephant through a crowd.
The king mounts a tamed one.
The best among people is the restrained one,
who endures insult. (321)

Tamed mules are excellent,
as are the well-bred horses of Sind,
and the great tusked elephants.
But more excellent than those
is a person who restrains himself. (322)

Certainly, not with these vehicles
could a person go to the unreached realm,
as a trained person goes
with restraint, with good self-control. (323)*

The elephant called "Guardian of the Treasure"
is hard to restrain when reeking with rut.

Bound, the elephant will not eat a morsel,
longing for the grove of elephants. (324)

When sluggish and stuffed,
sleeping, lying about, rolling around—
like a huge hog fed on fodder,
the lethargic person enters the womb again and again. (325)

Before, this mind would wander about
according to its pleasure,
as it wished, wherever it desired.
Now, I will keep it completely in check,
as a person holding a goad
controls a frenzied elephant. (326)

Delight in diligence!
Watch over your mind!
Pull yourselves out of misfortune
like an elephant, sunk in mud. (327)

If one could find a mature friend,
a companion who is wise, living productively,
he would overcome all dangers.
Let him go with that one, mindful and happy. (328)

If one cannot find a mature friend,
a companion who is wise, living productively,
let him go alone,
like a king abandoning conquered land,
like an elephant in the forest. (329)

A life of solitude is better—
there is no companionship with a childish person.
Let one go alone and do no damage,
having few cares, like an elephant in the forest. (330)

When need has arisen, friends are a comfort.
Contentment with whatever is, is a comfort.

When life is lost, merit is a comfort.
The abandonment of all pain is a comfort. (331)

A comfort in this world is loving your mother.
Loving your father is a comfort, too.
A comfort in this world is respect for a life of seeking.
Living a pure life is a comfort, too. (332)

A comfort is virtue into old age.
A comfort is the establishment of conviction.
A comfort is the attainment of insightful knowledge.
Not acting destructively is a comfort. (333)

{ Guide page 181 }

CHAPTER TWENTY-FOUR

Craving

तण्हावग्गो

The craving of a person who lives carelessly
grows like a creeping vine.
He plunges from existence to existence,
like a monkey seeking fruit in the forest.   (334)

Whomever this miserable craving,
this entanglement in the world, overcomes,
his sorrows grow, like grass well rained upon.   (335)

But whoever overcomes this miserable craving,
in this world so hard to overcome,
sorrows fall away from him,
like a drop of water from a lotus blossom.   (336)

I speak to you this auspicious word,
to all of you assembled here:
you must dig out the root of craving
as a person in need of roots pulls out the plant.
Do not let Māra break you again and again
as a stream breaks a reed.   (337)

As a cut tree grows back
if the root is undamaged and firm,
so too this pain emerges again and again
if the tendency toward craving is not rooted out.   (338)

The person whose thirty-six streams
flow mightily toward what is pleasing,
the currents—thoughts rooted in passion—
carry that person of wrong views away. (339)*

Streams always flow.
A plant, having sprouted, is still.
Seeing that plant arise,
you must cut its root with insight! (340)

Flowing, moistened
delights arise in a person.
Seeking ease, binding
themselves to pleasure,
these people undergo
birth and old age. (341)

Harassed by craving, people
scurry about like a hunted hare.
Bound by clinging and attachment,
they experience pain again and again
for a long time. (342)

Harassed by craving, people
scurry about like a hunted hare.
Therefore, let the practitioner,
longing to be free from passion,
dispel craving from himself. (343)

The person who is without cravings,
yet intent on the forest of desire,
who, freed from the forest of desire,
runs back to the forest of desire—
just look at that person:
released, he runs back into bondage. (344)

The wise say that the bond is not strong
that is made of iron, wood, or reed.

But the passionate longing for
jewelry, wives, and children—   (345)

this, say the wise, is a strong bond:
weighty, yielding, and hard to loosen.
Cutting even that, those who are without longing
wander, having abandoned
the pleasure of worldly desires.   (346)

Those who are affected by passion
fall into a torrent of their own making,
like a spider in its own web.
Cutting even that, the wise proceed without longing,
having abandoned all pain.   (347)

Let go of the past!
Let go of the future!
In the present, let go!
Gone to the other shore of becoming,
mind released entirely,
you will never again undergo
birth and old age.   (348)

For the person who is agitated by thoughts,
whose passions are severe,
who searches for the pleasurable,
craving grows all the more.
This person makes the bondage strong.   (349)

The person who delights
in the calming of thought,
meditates on the unpleasant,
constantly mindful—
this one will remove,
this one will cut,
the bond of Māra.   (350)*

The goal achieved, fearless,
free from craving, clear,
he destroys the sting of becoming.
This is his final embodiment.   (351)*

Free from craving, not grasping,
skilled in the interpretation of sentences,
he would understand the assemblage
of the words, from first to last.
He who has his final body,
possessing vast wisdom,
is called a "great person."   (352)

Overcoming all, knowing all, am I.
Unstained by all phenomena,
abandoning everything, released
at the dissolution of craving.
Having realized this myself,
whom could I teach?   (353)

The gift of the teaching surpasses every gift.
The flavor of the teaching surpasses every flavor.
Delight from the teaching surpasses all delight.
The dissolution of craving conquers every pain.   (354)

Possessions hurt the unthinking person,
but not those seeking the other shore.
Because of his craving for possessions,
the unthinking one hurts himself,
just as he hurts all others.   (355)

Weeds are the ruin of fields.
Passion is the ruin of this human world.
So, to those without passion,
what is given yields abundant fruit.   (356)

Weeds are the ruin of fields.
Hatred is the ruin of this human world.
So, to those without hatred,
what is given yields abundant fruit. (357)

Weeds are the ruin of fields.
Delusion is the ruin of this human world.
So, to those without delusion,
what is given yields abundant fruit. (358)

Weeds are the ruin of fields.
Yearning is the ruin of this human world.
So, to those without yearning,
what is given yields abundant fruit. (359)

{ *Guide page 183* }

CHAPTER TWENTY-FIVE

The Practitioner

भिक्खुवग्गो

Restraint of the eye is beneficial.
Beneficial is restraint of the ear.
Restraint of the nose is beneficial.
Beneficial is restraint of the tongue. (360)

Restraint of the body is beneficial.
Beneficial is restraint of speech.
Restraint of the mind is beneficial.
Beneficial is restraint all around.
Restrained all around, the practitioner
is released from all pain. (361)*

Hands restrained,
feet restrained,
voice restrained,
exercising the utmost restraint,
possessing inner delight,
composed, solitary, and content—
that person is called a "practitioner." (362)

The practitioner whose mouth is controlled,
who discusses the texts unassumingly,
explaining both the meaning and the spirit—
sweet is that one's speech. (363)

Taking pleasure in the teaching,
delighting in the teaching,
reflecting on the teaching,
bearing in mind the teaching,
the practitioner does not fall away
from the good way.   (364)

He should not demean his own achievement,
nor go about envying others.
The practitioner who is envious of others
cannot attain meditative concentration.   (365)

Even if he has achieved but little,
a practitioner should not demean
his own achievement.
The radiant ones praise that person
for his pure and vigorous life.   (366)

The person who has no sense of "mine"
anywhere in body and mind,
and who does not grieve for what is not—
that one is called a "practitioner."   (367)

Dwelling in loving kindness,
the practitioner who trusts in
the teaching of the Buddha
would reach the peaceful place:
the stilling of fabrication—ease.   (368)*

Bale out this boat, practitioner!
Baled out, it will go quickly for you.
Cutting off passion and aversion,
you will then reach the unbinding.   (369)

Five traits should be cut off,
five should be abandoned,
five should be further cultivated.

The practitioner who has gone beyond
the five attachments is called
"one who has crossed the flood."

(370)*

Meditate, practitioner!
Do not be negligent.
Do not let your mind go astray
in the twine of sensual pleasures.
Do not carelessly swallow a copper ball and,
burning, cry out, "This is pain!"

(371)

There is no meditation for the unwise.
There is no insight for the nonmeditator.
The person who meditates and has insight
is in the very presence of the unbinding.

(372)

For the practitioner whose mind is at peace,
who has entered into the empty place,
extraordinary delight arises
from perfect insight into the teaching.

(373)*

Thoroughly mastering the rise and fall
of the aggregates, from whatever source,
he attains delight and joy.
For those who understand,
this is the deathless.

(374)*

This is primary for an insightful practitioner:
guarding the senses, contentment,
restraint in line with the discipline,
association with friends who are encouraging,
who live a pure and vigorous life.

(375)*

He should be experienced in friendship.
He should be skillful in conduct.
Abounding in joy from that,
he will bring pain to an end.

(376)

As the jasmine sheds
its withered blossoms,
so should you, practitioners,
shed attachment and aversion.   (377)

At peace in body, in speech at peace,
at peace in mind, perfectly composed,
rejecting worldly possessions,
the practitioner is called
"one who is at peace."   (378)

You must exhort yourself,
you must examine yourself.
Being, with mindfulness,
guarded by you yourself,
you will dwell in ease, practitioner.   (379)

You, indeed, are the master of yourself.
You, indeed, are your own refuge.
So, restrain yourself,
like a merchant restrains a fine horse.   (380)

Abounding in joy,
the practitioner who trusts in
the teaching of the Buddha
would reach the peaceful place:
the stilling of fabrication—ease.   (381)

The young practitioner who engages
in the teaching of the Buddha
brightens this world
like the moon freed from a cloud.   (382)

{*Guide page 185*}

CHAPTER TWENTY-SIX

The Superior Person
ब्राह्मणवग्गो

Exerting yourself, cut the stream!
Dispel sensual pleasure, superior one!
Knowing the dissolution of the modes of fabrication,
you know the uncreated, superior one.   (383)*

When the superior person
has gone to the other shore
in the twofold practice,
then, for that one who knows,
all of his fetters disappear.   (384)*

For whom neither the far shore nor the near,
nor both the far and near, exists,
that person, free from fetters and distress,
I call superior.   (385)

Meditating, sitting clearly,
doing what had to be done,
free from the impulses,
the highest goal attained,
that person I call superior.   (386)

The sun is ablaze by day.
The moon shines at night.

The warrior is ablaze arrayed.
The superior one is ablaze meditating.
And every day and every night,
the awakened one is ablaze with splendor. (387)

It is because he keeps out the detrimental
that a person is superior.
It is because he lives peacefully,
that he is called a "seeker."
Sending forth toxins from himself,
he is therefore called "one who has gone forth." (388)*

A superior person should not assail
a superior person, nor should he berate him.
Shame on the person who assails a superior one!
Shame on the one who berates him! (389)

For a superior person, it is no insignificant matter
when restraining his mind from what is pleasing.
Whenever he turns away from the thought of injury,
then pain is appeased. (390)

One by whom no harm is done
with body, speech, or mind,
restrained in these three conditions,
that person I call superior. (391)

The person from whom might be learned
the teaching taught by the perfectly awakened one
should be respectfully honored,
as a Brahmin honors the sacrificial fire. (392)*

Not because of matted hair,
not by means of ancestry, not by birth
does a person become superior.
But because one is honest and just
he is at ease, he is superior. (393)*

What use is matted hair for you, unthinking one?
What use for you is deerskin clothing?
A dense thicket within you,
you groom yourself without.   (394)*

A person wearing dusty rags,
lean and veined,
meditating alone in the forest,
that one I call superior.   (395)

But I do not call him superior
who was born from his mother's womb
considered "superior."
That is just a person with possessions.
The one possessing nothing, given nothing,
that person I call superior.   (396)

The person who is not afraid,
having severed every tie,
transcending attachments, free,
that one I call superior.   (397)

Having cut off the strap and harness
together with the rope and the bridle,
lifting off the crossbar, awakened,
that is the person I call superior.   (398)

The innocent person who endures
insult, physical harm, and imprisonment,
whose strength is forbearance
—the strength of an army—
that one I call superior.   (399)

He who is without anger,
devout, virtuous, free from lust,
gentle, bearing his final body,
that person I call superior.   (400)

Like water on a lotus leaf,
like a mustard seed on a sharp point,
the person who does not stick to sensual pleasures,
that one I call superior.   (401)

The person who understands pain
dissolving it in this life by himself,
who has put down the burden and is free,
that one I call superior.   (402)

The person whose knowledge is profound,
who is wise, knowing which is the path
and which is not the path,
who has attained the highest goal,
that one I call superior.   (403)

The person who does not associate
with either householders or mendicants,
living free from attachments, desiring little,
that one I call superior.   (404)

The person who has lain down violence
toward sentient beings—plants and animals—
who neither kills nor causes to kill,
that one I call superior.   (405)

The person who is harmonious amid the hostile,
peaceful amid the violent,
free from grasping amid the greedy,
that one I call superior.   (406)

The person whose passion and aversion,
pride and pretense have fallen
like a mustard seed off a sharp point,
that one I call superior.   (407)

The person who would speak in a way
that is gentle, instructive, and honest,

speech with which he would offend no one,
that one I call superior.

(408)

The person in this world
who would not take what is not given,
whether large or small, light or heavy,
beautiful or ugly,
that one I call superior.

(409)

The person for whom there are no expectations
concerning either this world or the world beyond,
who is without wishing, free,
that one I call superior.

(410)

The person for whom there are no attachments,
who, because of his insight, is free from doubt,
who has attained immersion into the deathless,
that one I call superior.

(411)

The person who has gone beyond
attachment to both gain and loss,
who is without sorrow, clear and pure,
that one I call superior.

(412)

Clear and pure as the moon,
luminous, serene,
the delight for existence exhausted,
that one I call superior.

(413)

The person who has traversed this difficult, muddy path—
the bewilderment that is the swirl of becoming—
the meditator who has crossed over, reached the other shore,
free from desire, free from doubt, not grasping, unbound,
that one I call superior.

(414)

The person who, desires abandoned,
would wander without a home,

the desire for existence exhausted,
that one I call superior.   (415)

The person who, craving abandoned,
would wander without a home,
the craving for existence exhausted,
that one I call superior.   (416)

Having renounced the human bond,
the person who, gone beyond the divine bond,
is loosened from all bonds,
that one I call superior.   (417)

Having renounced likes and dislikes, cooled,
without a foundation for further existence,
a hero who has overcome the entire world,
that one I call superior.   (418)

The person who thoroughly understands
the death and birth of beings,
who is unattached, well gone, awakened,
that one I call superior.   (419)

The person whose destination
the radiant ones, spirits, and humans do not know,
the accomplished one who has dissolved the impulses,
that one I call superior.   (420)

The person for whom there is nothing
in the beginning, middle, or end,
who, having nothing, is free from grasping,
that one I call superior.   (421)

The person who is fearless, excellent,
heroic, a great sage, victorious,
free from desire, cleansed, awakened,
that one I call superior.   (422)

The person who knows his former lives
and sees the high and low states of existence,
who has reached the end of births,
the sage who has perfected knowledge—
has perfected all that is to be perfected—
that one I call superior.

(423)

{ Guide page 188 }

Guide to
Reading the Text

Introduction

GENRE, USE, AND THEMES

What is everywhere passes unnoticed. Nothing is more commonplace than the experience of reading, and nothing is less well-known. Reading is taken for granted to such an extent that at first glance it seems nothing need be said about it.[1]

If we pause to consider the process by which we arrive at an understanding of a particular Buddhist text, Tzvetan Todorov's words ring true as both warning and promise. For students of Buddhism in the twenty-first century, the understanding of Buddhism itself has been almost exclusively dependent on reading. Yet our reading practices often pass unnoticed. In this section I would like to explore how we might become more self-conscious about the way we read Buddhist literature.

What kind of work is the *Dhammapada*? To answer this question we must consider the genre, use, and themes of a Buddhist text. These are closely related. In an ancient ninefold classification system of Buddhist literature, the *Dhammapada* was categorized as *gāthā*, or a verse text. What does that designation signify? Some scholars have unhelpfully taken it to mean that the *Dhammapada* is a work of poetry. In fact, one of the most serious of all scholars to work on the text had the following to say. (Please bear in mind that I repeat this as a way of discouraging the reader from making a similar, well, error.)

Now and then a monk might be a poet, and here and there among the Dharmapada [the Sanskrit spelling] verses we have the good fortune to inherit some fragments of excellent poetry. But we should not expect to find very much. Poetry is not an easy art, and good poets are always rare. To build from other men's bricks and sanctified clichés is tolerably simple; and many a monk entirely devoid of poetic ability was readily persuaded that his verses were no worse than those of his neighbor.

The resulting vast accumulations of insipid mediocrity which piety preserves are by no means peculiar to Buddhism.[2]

If we challenge the premise that the verses of the *Dhammapada* are "poetry," most of this criticism becomes moot. (I assume that for the author of this quotation, the English term "poetry" refers to what corresponds to Sanskrit *kāvya*, that is, ornate or fine verse. I base this assumption on the fact that he elsewhere juxtaposes the monk's "poetry" and "great religious art and literature.") Although *gāthā* may, in *certain* instances, be translated as "poetry," the *Dhammapada* should not in fact be read as "poetry." *Gāthā* refers simply to either sections of larger texts or independent works that were composed in verse meters, as distinct from nonmetrical prose. In most instances, there is evidence that this form was intended to facilitate memorization. It should be remembered that until the first century C.E. or so, Buddhist "literature" was composed, transmitted, and stored orally. Even the prose sections of the Pāli canon contain one mnemonic device after another—stock formulas, reiterated statements, lists, numbered sequences, extensive passage repetition, transferable templates, and others—toward this end.

Metered, rhythmic verse is an even better way to create ease of memorization. The Buddha himself addressed this issue in a passage revealing a grave danger to the preservation of his teachings in the future— the danger of *mere poetry:*

> When those discourses spoken by [me] that are deep, deep in meaning, supramundane, dealing with emptiness, are being recited, [practitioners in the future] will not be eager to listen to them, nor lend an ear to them, nor apply their minds to understand them; and they will not think those teachings should be studied and mastered. But when those discourses that are mere poetry composed by poets, beautiful in words and phrases . . . are being recited, they will be eager to listen

to them. . . . In this way, those discourses spoken by [me] that are deep, deep in meaning, supramundane, dealing with emptiness, will disappear. (*Saṃyuttanikāya* 2.20.7)

If these verses are not poetry, as the Buddha would hope, what are they? To answer this question, we have to consider the *Dhammapada*'s purpose, which can be stated simply. The text is intended for instruction, encouragement, and propagation. It constitutes a structured summation of the salient points of Buddhist teachings. Nuns, monks, and laypeople alike would have heard the text recited by a teacher; memorized it themselves in part or whole; invoked it for auspicious-making ends; recited it for didactic ends; quoted it in debate, public lectures, and sermons; perused it for recall of some point or issue. Its greatest use, I can imagine, was as a constant reminder of what is important in life.

Many readers of the *Dhammapada,* scholarly and otherwise, have expressed doubt that there is a coherent thematic structure to the work. But I would suggest that the reader really does not have to look further than the table of contents for a guide to thematic structure (though in the Pāli original the "table of contents" comes at the end of the text).

As is common with most Indian spiritual traditions, the approach to a well-lived life is gradual but steady, "like the gentle sloping of the ocean's floor," as the Buddha said of his path. The *Dhammapada* itself reveals this approach by proceeding thematically along the path delineated by the Buddha. It begins by asking the reader to consider the primacy of the very mind that is reading—seeking, perceiving, reflecting on, judging—the words before him or her. Is it clear, or is it muddy? This is a good place to begin since, as the Buddha observed, mind—awareness, cognizance—is where our life, and hence our predicament, unfolds. Where else?

After this foundational theme of Buddhist teaching, which, not coincidentally, is also the foundation of experience, has been established, the reader is reminded, in the following chapter, of the importance of diligence in pursuing his or her "spiritual" enterprise. It is a blunt reminder.

> Diligence is the path to the deathless.
> Negligence is the path of death.
> The diligent do not die.

> Those who are negligent
> are as the dead.

One of the Buddha's favorite metaphors for religious practice is "cultivation." This is, for instance, one of the terms that is translated as "meditation," *bhāvanā*. Given the ubiquity of farms and fields in India, such an agricultural image is doubly apt. No matter how damaged a field may be, it can be improved and enriched—cultivated—to produce a favorable harvest. While it is true that anyone may attempt this cultivation, not everyone will succeed. This is because cultivation requires specific skills.

By positioning the chapter on diligence at the outset, the *Dhammapada* makes clear the crucial necessity of acquiring this particular skill *at the beginning*. It is a warning that the promise of the text will be unfulfilled without sustained effort. This is also a clear signal to the reader about the nature of the work, as well as the nature of reading it. With this reorientation toward what is primary in both experience and attitude, the text is able to begin again, at the beginning. It returns to the mind. *Now*, perhaps, we are prepared to acknowledge that what stands at the beginning—the first instance of our lived experience—is a mind that is "trembling," "quivering," so "difficult to guard and hard to restrain."

Chapter by chapter the text reveals the matters the Buddha considered essential: the nature of the self, the value of relationships, the importance of moment-to-moment awareness, the destructiveness of anger, the ambiguity of the world's beauty, the inevitability of aging and physical decay, and the certainty of death. Will you emulate the impulsive, immature, childish person, or will you acquire real skill and become accomplished—*simply as a person?*

Hindrances to accomplishment are pointed out at every turn. Some of those that are underscored through their frequent recurrence are poor self-restraint in body, speech, and thoughts; the tendency toward anger and irritability; the inability to cultivate mindfulness; the failure to distinguish between detrimental and beneficial modes of being; the lack of sustained effort. To balance these all-too-human traits, the text also at every turn points to applicable methods that lead the practitioner away from these traits and toward the human virtuosity known as awakening. The two methods most frequently mentioned or alluded to—because they are most central to the early Buddhist way—are meditation and mindfulness. Concerning the importance of these practices, the Buddha said this:

> No other thing do I know that brings so much harm as a mind that is untamed, unguarded, unprotected, and uncontrolled. Such a mind truly brings harm.
> No other thing do I know that brings so much benefit as a mind that is tamed, guarded, protected, and controlled. Such a mind truly brings great benefit. (*Anguttaranikāya* 1.4.1–10 selected)

Finally, the *Dhammapada* ends by giving an account of the view from the conclusion of the way, the destination that has provided the orientation for the entire text. The person who stands here, on "the other shore," is one who is *superior*. But to the Buddha, superiority is not achieved by virtue of privileged birth, as was the view in his day. It is instead a designation for *anyone* who has "attained immersion into the deathless" and thereby become serene, unagitated, and free of dust.

PLACE IN BUDDHIST LITERATURE

The *Dhammapada* occupies a relatively humble position in the grand scheme of Buddhist literature. That a great communal recitation was held immediately after the death of the Buddha (ca. 400 B.C.E.)[3] is undisputed among the three schools, or "vehicles," of Buddhism, Theravāda (ca. 400 B.C.E. to the present), Mahāyāna (ca. 100 B.C.E. to the present), and Vajrayāna (ca. 700 C.E. to the present). The purpose of this first council, attended by some five hundred monks, was to agree upon, and thereby fix, the wording of what the Buddha had always referred to as his *dhammavinaya,* teachings and communal regulations. According to the Theravāda—prevalent in Sri Lanka, Thailand, Laos, Cambodia, and Burma—the basic organization of the Buddha's "dispensation" (*sāsana*) was also established at this council in northeastern India. A term evoking gathering, holding, and preserving was used to refer to the two divisions: "basket" (*piṭaka*). In this manner, the two great collections, *dhammapiṭaka* and *vinayapiṭaka,* were established. Two hundred or so years later, a third basket was added. This division included collections of further analysis and clarification of the teachings by early followers of the Buddha; hence, it is called the *Abhidhammapiṭaka,* "basket of elaborations on the teachings."

An abbreviated map of the Theravāda canon thus looks like this:

1. *Vinayapiṭaka.* The rules and regulations governing the details of monastic life.
2. *Suttapiṭaka.* The teachings of the Buddha in the form of dialogues, discussions, and talks. Subdivided into five sections:
   a. *Dīghanikāya.* The "collection of long" discourses. This contains thirty-four lengthy *suttas* that, in many ways, serve as an introduction to the teachings.[4]
   b. *Majjhimanikāya.* The "collection of middle-length" discourses. This section contains 152 *suttas.*
   c. *Saṃyuttanikāya.* The "collection of connected" discourses. The 2,904 *suttas* of this section are among the most thorough and penetrating of Buddhist literature. These texts presuppose on the side of the interlocutor extensive experience in the study and practice of the teachings.
   d. *Aṅguttaranikāya.* The "collection of numerical" discourses. The 2,344 *suttas* in this section are more or less summative.
   e. *Kuddakanikāya.* The "collection of small" books. This section comprises fifteen individual works that are held to have been added to the *piṭaka* later than the other collections. All these works are of anonymous authorship. The best known of them in the West are the *Jātaka,* the *Theragāthā,* and the *Therīgāthā.* The *Dhammapada* is the second work of this collection.
3. *Abhidhammapiṭaka.* The "basket of elaborations on the teachings." This group consists of seven works that examine aspects of the *sutta* material in minute detail. It is unfortunate that the *Abhidhamma* is routinely referred to in the West as "philosophy." The abiding concern of these texts is to understand the nature of psychological-physical being as a means of realizing freedom from the painful restrictions that this being entails. And that is just what the Buddha said it is: diagnosis and therapy. Is *this* a concern of philosophy as it is practiced in the West today?

APPROACHING THE *DHAMMAPADA*

The *Dhammapada* was one of the first Buddhist works to be translated into Western languages. Since its initial appearance in 1855—in Latin!—the work has been rendered numerous times into English alone. Much like the earliest communities of Buddhists, modern Western readers have apparently been captivated by the relative ease of access that the *Dhammapada* affords to difficult Buddhist doctrines. I have benefited greatly from many of these translations and do not wish to denigrate any of them. But I think it would not be unfair to insist that many of them should be considered as pioneering works that, having served the reading public well for many decades or longer, may now be replaced by fresh renderings. The language, syntax, diction, and style of these older translations evoke a time and place other than our own.

The most visible and widely read of the English translations is the 1973 Penguin Classics version by Juan Mascaró.[5] Because of its consistent popularity, this version has certainly had some impact on the spread of Buddhism in North America. (In fact, my own introduction to Buddhism in 1975 was through this very work.) As beautiful and sympathetic as it is, however, there are two serious shortcomings to Mascaró's translation (these shortcomings may be seen as representing the first of three kinds of approaches to *Dhammapada* translation; the other two then follow).

First, in his lengthy introduction, Mascaró contextualized the *Dhammapada* in what has become, for most serious readers, an outdated Perennial Philosophy framework.[6] Even thirty years ago this approach misrepresented the Buddhist understanding of the work; today, it presents an obstacle of implausibility to the intelligent, informed reader. Again, this approach may engender a powerful, even convincing, presentation of ideas and verse, but only at the expense of their real force—as *Buddhist* ideas and verse. The second problem with Mascaró's version is that his translation is too often grammatically and doctrinally inaccurate. Since he was, in fact, knowledgeable in Sanskrit and Pāli, I assume that this inaccuracy stems from Mascaró's apparent philosophical commitment to perennialism: too often he prodded the text to say what he needed and wanted it to say.

Another, in many ways opposite, approach to the *Dhammapada* is that represented by the few (I can think of only three) English translations that serve as reliable correctives to the grammatical and doctrinal imprecision, and antiquated language, of other versions. The authors of these translations, outstanding scholars of Buddhism, have chosen accuracy over aesthetics and thus, to some extent, have sacrificed readability to grammatical precision. (Two of these translations are so precise that it would be possible to produce virtually the actual Pāli version of the text from the English.) To the nonacademic reader, these works can thus appear dry, even perhaps lifeless.

The third mode of translation I would like to mention is that of the practitioner-scholar. Some of these works are by Southeast Asians writing in English, some are translations from Thai, Singhalese, et cetera, still others are by Westerners who have trained in Theravāda communities. As might be expected, these represent some of the most illuminating and penetrating translations. Over the years of reading the *Dhammapada*, however, I could see one area for improvement even here. (I'll say it in parentheses to soften the tone of my impertinence: these translations can come across as *too revealing*.)

In most such cases, the strategy adopted for elucidating a verse is to refer to the later Pāli commentarial tradition. These commentaries were produced by monks in the leading Buddhist institutions of their day as a way, in part, to fix the text and provide authoritative interpretation. As such, these works are by turn penetrative and pedantic, constructive and conservative. They are, furthermore, records of quite particular, historically situated, understandings of the text. Reading back in the distant horizon of a text is, of course, quite fascinating. But what was said there can also be beside the point. Now I am assuming things about the reader and what he or she takes to be "the point"; and this assumption obliges me to explain my own approach to translating the *Dhammapada*, which is centered on the reader in the room.

THE READER IN THE ROOM

The dawn of the *Dhammapada* broke in the actual utterances of the Buddha nearly twenty-five hundred years ago. Its horizon began to open up with the particular fashioning of these—plus, most certainly, contemporary additions—into the work we have come to know as the *Dhammapada*, or its Sanskrit equivalent, *Dharmapada*. This horizon expanded with each generation's attempt to understand the text, and to make it relevant to its particular life situation. Now, after eighty-some generations of hearing, reading, commenting on, debating, editing, and living the verses, the horizon reaches us here, today. So, my assumption is that you, the reader, are interested in what these verses might have to say to *you*. The text lies before you at a very particular point in its immense horizon: *now, now, what will you do with it?* Another way of asking this is: *What's the point?*

For the reader whom the *Dhammapada* envisions, the point—that is, the purpose and significance of engaging the text now *at all*—is to do the spadework of making sense of the verses through a *careful and diligent* investigation of the matters they address. The reader should seek the meaning of these verses as a skilled gardener gathers flowers.

> Who will master this earth,
> this world of death and radiant beings?
> Who will gather a well-taught verse on the way,
> as a skilled gardener gathers a flower?

> A seeker will master this earth,
> this world of death and radiant beings.
> A seeker will gather a well-taught verse on the way,
> as a skilled gardener gathers a flower.

In ancient India, flowers, and flowering trees, creepers, herbs, and bushes, whether gracing well-manicured gardens or abounding in forest, jungle, or field, were universally loved and praised. Classical Sanskrit poetry is routinely "ornamented" by the scent, luster, and beauty evoked by flower imagery. Imagine now an *unskilled* gardener gathering such fine things. What becomes of the flowers? What becomes of their scent, luster, and beauty? It is not difficult to transfer this metaphor to the reading of the verses themselves. Gathering the flowers that are the verses requires skill. Furthermore, gathering the flowers—reading the verses—is not enough.

> As a bee flying from a flower,
> having taken up its nectar,
> does not harm its luster or fragrance,

So must the reader—the seeker—read each verse: by extracting its meaning. The Buddha himself used the metaphors of extraction and distillation to describe his teachings:

> Just as the ocean has a single flavor, the flavor of salt, so this teaching
> has a single flavor, the flavor of freedom. (*Aṅguttaranikāya* 8.19)

How is this delicate alchemical task achieved? The quick answer, already given, is to become "skilled." Virtually every verse of the *Dhammapada* describes the traits, dispositions, qualities, and ways of being that a person must embody if he or she would attain freedom from the pain of human existence (Pāli *nibbāna,* Sanskrit *nirvāṇa*), the ultimate goal of the Buddha's way. So, if the nectar of the text is freedom, then the scent, luster, and beauty of each verse in the garden of the *Dhammapada* is *skill.*

This is where most readers require assistance. One solution, as mentioned previously, is to let the authoritative commentators of the past provide the assistance. There is an astute understanding of human psychology behind this move of the ancient commentators. For a concerned and responsible reader will *naturally* supply his or her own running commentary. This is what is sometimes referred to as the "readerly" nature of a work. The reader brings to bear on the text his or her imagination, concerns, needs, dreams, disappointments, et cetera, and thus, in the very process of reading, contributes to the writing.

As the commentators, and those who utilize them, recognize, there is a real danger in being left to one's own devices with the *Dhammapada.* Much of the language is technical. That is, the Buddhist usage of a term often carries quite specific connotations, nuances, and allusions, even an altogether innovative denotation. So, when you read "mind," you need to know what the Buddha was referring to, rather than assume, as we so often do, that you already know.

My solution to this problem is as follows. Whenever a technical term is used, alluded to, or even just presupposed, I provide an explanatory note (such verses are marked with asterisks). But unlike in the works mentioned earlier, my source of light is not the commentaries. Other than an occasional citation of a secondary source, or a brief word from a contemporary author, I have exclusively referred to and quoted from the canonical *suttas,* the presumed earliest discourses of the Buddha. The purpose of this solution is to provide the reader with the minimal, though necessary, conceptual apparatus for thinking through the verses on his or her own. A merit of this apparatus is that it locates the *Dhammapada* in the "thought-world" of an early strata of the teachings, close to, if not virtually identical with, its own.

My hope is that this method will create a clearer view, enabling the reader to fuse his or her present horizon with that of an earlier moment in the life of the text. Such "fusions" will require further work on the part of the reader.[7] To read the text properly, as its numerous internal signals indicate, the reader will have to follow the leads provided in the notes and plunge more deeply into the *suttas* directly.[8] The apparatus, furthermore, is devoid of discussion of grammatical problems and other textual-linguistic issues. Not only is such discussion unnecessary for the intended readership but it has already been masterfully achieved by other scholars.[9] In addition to the explanatory notes, I have provided a short overview to each chapter. This is my way of suggesting, via a synopsis of the verses themselves, an orientation for reading the verses.

A COMMENT ON THE TRANSLATION

In my actual translation of the *Dhammapada,* I have attempted to follow the Buddha's dictum of seeking the middle way between extremes. Thus, I have sought to produce an English rendering that is neither too loose nor too tight. By "too loose" I mean a translation that strays from the original language. The reader can be confident that the English says what the Pāli says. By the same token, I have produced a work *in English.* To do this, I have had to deal with some features of the Pāli language that work against English usages. My solutions to some of these problems are as follows:

- In a few instances the rules of Pāli meter require a present verb tense where a future seems to be indicated. I alter this accordingly.
- In some cases I translate the third-person optative verb as either a second-person optative or an imperative. For example, "One should regard the person who sees one's faults as a revealer of treasures" becomes "Regard the person who sees your faults as a revealer of treasures."
- Concerning gender pronouns, the Pāli invariably uses "he" or some other masculine form. I experimented with mixing these with feminine forms, but this mixture only produced confusion. I hope that the retention of masculine forms will not detract too much from my goal of allowing the text to speak to contemporary readers. I have tried to ameliorate this bias somewhat by sometimes using feminine forms in the chapter introductions and the endnotes. So I hope that female readers of this translation will consider themselves included in the verses.
- In a few cases, a second-person optative ("You should make an effort") is translated as an imperative ("Make an effort!").

More significant than these changes are several renderings that a more experienced reader of Buddhist literature will find unusual. In every case, such a deviation from common practice is explained in the endnotes. I will mention the three most obvious instances only briefly here; it is more effective to examine them in context. Again, in the notes I explain in some detail my reasoning for these changes.

- *Nibbāna/nirvāṇa* is translated as "unbinding."
- *Dhamma* is translated in multiple ways in order to capture its numerous meanings: "teaching," "way," "quality," "phenomenon," and so on.
- All designations of specific types of followers in the Buddha's day (monks, mendicants, ascetics, et cetera) are rendered in terms such as "practitioner," "seeker," and so on.

My hope behind all of these issues has been to produce a translation that is simultaneously historically responsible and pertinent to the present day. I have tried to retain the Buddhist ambience and understanding of the work by preserving the aesthetic, philosophical heft, and psychological principles of the original. At the same time, I have sought to capture for the twentieth-first-century reader the vibrancy and relevance that have endeared the *Dhammapada* to countless "seekers of the other shore."

NOTES TO THE INTRODUCTION

1. Tzvetan Todorov, *Genres in Discourse* (Cambridge: Cambridge University Press, 1990), p. 39.
2. John Brough, *The Gāndhārī Dharmapada* (London: Oxford University Press, 1962), p. xvii.
3. The Buddha's dates are usually given as 563–483 B.C.E., but the research of the eminent German scholar Heinz Bechert and others shows convincingly that these should be adjusted forward. See Heinz Bechert, ed., *The Dating of the Historical Buddha,* Symposien zur Buddhismusforschung, vol. 4, pt. 1 (Göttingen: Vanderhoeck und Ruprecht, 1991). Bechert's "Introductory Essay: The Scope of the Symposium and the Question of Methodology" (pp. 1–21) provides a helpful summary of the complex issues involved in Indian chronology. See also his "The Date of the Buddha—An Open Question of Ancient Indian History" in the same volume (pp. 222–236). In brief, Bechert holds that the Buddha's death occurred shortly before Alexander the Great's invasion of India, "i.e., between ca. 400 B.C. and ca. 350 B.C." (p. 236).

4. For a detailed account of this theory, see Joy Manné, "Categories of Sutta in the Pāli Nikāyas and Their Implications for Our Appreciation of the Buddhist Teaching and Literature," *Journal of the Pali Text Society* 15 (1990): 29–87.

5. Juan Mascaró, *The Dhammapada: The Path of Perfection* (New York: Penguin Books, 1973).

6. "Perennial Philosophy" is a term coined by Aldous Huxley in his popular anthology of "sacred" literature, *The Perennial Philosophy* (London: Chatto and Windus, 1946). As the term itself indicates, the basic thesis of Huxley's book, and of the subsequent school of thought subscribing to that thesis, is that all religions, regardless of their cultural, historical, and linguistic peculiarities, possess a "Highest Common Factor." This common denominator is the "chemically pure state" of the tradition. This "same essential indescribable Fact" is the Perennial Philosophy, or *philosophia perennis,* because it appears repeatedly throughout history, "now partial, now complete, now in this form, now in that, again and again."

Although Mascaró is not explicit about this, his perennialist leanings are apparent in his use of wide-ranging literature to show the universal nature of the truths expressed in the *Dhammapada*. He quotes, for instance, from traditions and authors as divergent as Kabir, St. Teresa, the Bhagavadgītā, Rumi, Rabindranath Tagore, Jesus, Shelley, Keats, the Upaniṣads, the Tao Te Ching, Zen, and Shakespeare. The overall effect is meant to reveal that the "infinite Light" to which the Buddha awoke is the same light informing every "spiritual leader" of past, present, and future.

The reader may in fact find the perennialist thesis attractive, even convincing. My point is only that it serves as a poor framework to explicate Buddhist literature.

7. On the idea of "the fusion of horizons," see Hans-Georg Gadamer, *Truth and Method* (1960; New York: Continuum, 1994), in particular, pages 306–307.

8. The translations of canonical works that I quote in the individual chapter introductions and endnotes are as follows. (I have occasionally made, in reference to the Pāli texts of the *Nikāyas,* slight alterations to these translations; but I have not further burdened the notes with reference to those editions.) Maurice Walshe, *The Long Discourses of the Buddha: A Translation of the Dīgha Nikāya* (1987; Boston: Wisdom Publications, 1995); Bhikkhu Ñāṇamoli and Bhikkhu Bodhi, *The Middle Length Discourses of the Buddha: A Translation of the Majjhima Nikāya* (1995; Boston: Wisdom Publications, 2001); Bhikkhu Bodhi, *The Connected Discourses of the Buddha: A Translation of the Saṃyutta Nikāya* (Boston: Wisdom Publications, 2000); Nyanaponika Thera and Bhikkhu Bodhi, *Numerical Discourses of the Buddha: An Anthology of Suttas from the Aṅguttara Nikāya* (Walnut Creek, Calif.: AltaMira Press, 1999).

The *suttas* should not be viewed as arcane texts out of reach to the average student of Buddhism. A thorough grounding in this literature is particularly important in an environment such as twenty-first-century North America, where the lure of an eclectic approach to and passing acquaintance with Buddhist material is so great.

9. See K. R. Norman, *The Word of the Doctrine* (*Dhammapada*) (Oxford: Pali Text Society, 1997), and John Ross Carter and Mahinda Palihawadana, *The Dhammapada* (Oxford: Oxford University Press, 1987). To give the reader an idea of the scope of Carter and Palihawadana's ambitious and important work, I quote from the "subtitle": "a new English translation with the Pali text and the first English translation of the commentary's explanation of the verses with notes translated from the Sinhala sources and the critical textual comments."

The present translation is based on the Pāli edition prepared by O. von Hinüber and K. R. Norman, *Dhammapada* (Oxford: Pali Text Society, 1995). This edition includes the comprehensive word index compiled by Shoko Tabata and Tetsuya Tabata. All translations of other canonical works are those of the authors mentioned in note 8, unless otherwise indicated.

Chapter Overviews and Notes

⎯⎯ ৩৩ ⎯⎯

CHAPTER ONE

CONTRASTING PAIRS

यमकवग्गो

The *Dhammapada* begins at the beginning: with that human capacity for awareness commonly called "the mind." What, within the range of actual human experience, could possibly precede one's mind? Objects may lie "out there," in the world, but it is the individual's mind that produces the specific fashioning or appearance that constitutes his or her lived world. This process of fashioning is what accounts for the myriad viewpoints that people inevitably bring to the shared experience of a given event or, more to the point, to their shared observation of anything seen, heard, smelled, tasted, felt, or thought. Because of the importance of the mind in giving shape to what lies before our sense faculties, the first verse of the *Dhammapada* reminds the reader to consider the quality of his or her very mind. Is your mind filled (polluted) with views and opinions and presuppositions that may actually hinder an understanding of what follows? Or is it in a state that supports understanding—open, seeking, clear, and pure?

The chapter lays out a simple ethical polarity. This is the significance of the title, "Contrasting Pairs." One possibility: act, speak, and think in productive ways, and things will go well for you. The other possibility: act, speak, and think in destructive ways, and things will go poorly for you. The choice is yours.

This chapter also introduces several key themes that will recur throughout the *Dhammapada*. These too are presented as opposites. On the one hand, there is the profoundly transformative effect on a person's life and environment of the following qualities: calmness and peace; bodily, verbal, and mental restraint; the forgoing of transient sense pleasure; and the continual cultivation of productive qualities. On the other hand, there are the damaging effects of hostility, lack of restraint, the yielding to the impulse toward transient pleasure, and the failure to cultivate beneficial qualities. The important psychological and ethical category of the "stain" is introduced here, as well as the notion of consequence, both in this life and those beyond.

NOTES
(TO VERSES IN THE TRANSLATION WITH ASTERISKS)

1–2. *Preceded by mind are phenomena.* The Buddha taught that human life is properly lived within the range of immediate experience. This may seem obvious, but a central contention of Buddhism is that we are constantly wandering outside that range, into the improper, detrimental range of storytelling, fantasy, and fabrication. Verse 21 will teach us that, although it is possible to be careless or inattentive regarding what appears to our eyes, ears, nose, tongue, body, and mind, to do so is to be as good as dead. A story told by the Buddha bears this same message:

> Once a hawk suddenly swooped down on a quail and seized it. Then the quail, as it was being carried off by the hawk, lamented, "O just my bad luck and lack of merit that I was wandering out of my proper range and into the territory of others! If only I had kept to my proper range today, to my own ancestral territory, this hawk would have been no match for me in battle." . . . This is what happens to anyone who wanders into what is not his proper range. (*Saṃyuttanikāya* 5.47.6, translation by Thanissaro Bhikkhu, *The Wings to Awakening* [Barre, Mass.: Dhamma Dana Publications, 1996], pp. 96–97)

Immediate experience is not only our "proper range," it is, if we are honest about the manner in which our lives unfold moment by moment, our *only* range—it is *all* there is. The Buddha, in fact, used the term "the all" (*sabba*) to denote this range:

> I will teach you the all. . . . The eye and forms, the ear and sounds, the nose and odors, the tongue and tastes, the body and tactile objects, the mind and mental phenomena. This is called the all. If anyone should speak thus:

"Having rejected this all, I will make known another all"—that would be a mere empty boast on his part. If he were questioned he would not be able to reply and, further, he would meet with vexation. For what reason? Because that would not be within his domain. (*Saṃyuttanikāya* 4.35.23)

It is important to note here the phrase "the mind and mental phenomena." In the West, we do not normally consider the mind to be a sense faculty, comparable to the ear, or a thought to be an object of sense, such as a sound. But that is precisely the case here. For this reason, the term "phenomena" in the statement "preceded by mind are phenomena" could be correctly rendered as "mental objects." That is, just as an ear has the capacity to "touch" (*phassa*) sounds, the capacity of mind is precisely to touch thoughts, or mental objects. But mind (*manas*) has a capacity that exceeds those of the other five sense organs. The Buddha expressed this as follows.

These five faculties have different domains, different resorts; they do not experience one another's resort and domain. What five? The eye faculty, the ear faculty, the nose faculty, the tongue faculty, the body faculty. Now, these five faculties having different domains, different resorts, not experiencing one another's resort and domain—they take recourse in the mind, and the mind experiences their resort and domain.

(*Saṃyuttanikāya* 5.48.42)

The mind partakes in the experience of the other five sensory modes: it *gets involved* in seeing, hearing, tasting, et cetera, by classifying, judging, conceptualizing—that is, to a great extent, by coloring and forming—the naked experience of what appears before the eye, ear, nose, tongue, and body. It is with this more extensive capacity of mind in play that the translation reads "phenomena." (For this reason, too, mind is sometimes excluded from the list of faculties. See notes 7–8 and 13–14.)

1–2. *pain...ease.* These terms translate the central Buddhist conception of *dukkha* and its opposite, *sukha*. The most common renderings of these terms are "suffering" and "happiness." Both of these English words, however, are too drastic and too final to capture the Buddhist views behind *dukkha* and *sukha*. Probably very few people would characterize their lives as being bound up in persistent *suffering*. But many would, perhaps, admit to the kind of pervasive unsatisfactoriness of lived experience that the Buddhist term *dukkha* conveys. For instance, we all know that even a "happy" moment fades away; and in that gap between the experience of happiness and its fading is felt the sting, however subtle, of dissatisfaction. And since our lives are successions of such moments, pain is said to be "pervasive." But Buddhists would go still further, to the point of what appears paradoxical, even contradictory: it is not only in the gap that *dukkha* is present but even in the very experience of happiness.

The Buddha said repeatedly that he teaches one thing, and one thing only: pain and its ending. His entire teaching, as well as his career as a teacher, begins with the formulation of the four noble truths: (1) pain; (2) the origin of pain (craving); (3) the cessation of pain (unbinding, *nibbāna/nirvāna*; see note 23); and (4) the path leading to the cessation of pain (the eightfold path) (see notes 11–12, 38, 190, and 191). The first noble truth, *dukkha*, holds that every moment of our lives is pervaded by a persistent tinge of discomfort, dissatisfaction, lack of ease, *pain*. The fundamental reason for this painful shading of existence is that all phenomena are "marked" by impermanence and nonsubstantiality (see note 62).

It is important to point out that the Buddha held that this and the second noble truth are observable facts of existence, rather than mere metaphysical theories that must be accepted as articles of faith. The point is not to *believe in* their validity, it is to *see* them as they unfold in our lives. The first, pervasive pain, "is to be fully understood"; the second, pain's origin, craving, "is to be abandoned"; the third, its cessation, unbinding or *nibbāna/nirvāna*, "is to be realized"; and the fourth, the path to cessation, "is to be developed." As many have noted, this scheme conforms to the basic medical model of disease, diagnosis, prognosis, and prescription. (On the four noble truths, see the section of the *Saṃyuttanikāya* known as the first discourse of the Buddha, "Setting in Motion the Wheel of the Doctrine," 5.56.11.)

In reading the *Dhammapada*, it is important to keep in mind the fact that the Buddha is not addressing the concerns we in the West normally expect from religious teachers. He has no interest whatsoever in giving his listeners (and now readers) answers to questions about creator gods, or about beginnings and ends of the cosmos.

There are at least two reasons for this stance: (1) these questions involve such a "thicket" of presuppositions, speculations, unexamined views, unsupportable opinions, et cetera (about, for example, the nature of self and reality, and the relationship of the two) as to be virtually meaningless and literally unanswerable; and (2) knowing the answer—or really *believing* or *accepting* someone else's *view*—"does not lead to disenchantment, to dispassion, to cessation, to peace, to direct knowledge, to awakening, to *nibbāna*" (see *Majjhimanikāya* 72). So, according to the Buddha, the great religious and philosophical questions of humanity "miss the mark," are "to remain unanswered," and should thus "be set aside." In short, the Buddha

valued inquiry, investigation, and discovery and insight over dogmatic asser-
tion and unexamined belief. (See also *Aṅguttaranikāya* 3.65 and *Majjhimanikāya* 47.)

5. *an interminable truth.* These are strong words for a Buddhist. The possibility
of there being entities and truths (*dhamma* in the text) that are eternal, everlasting, foundational, and absolute (*sanantano*), while routinely posited by
theistic systems such as Hinduism and Christianity, is denied by the Buddha
(on the basis of *anattā* and *anicca*—nonsubstantiality and impermanence).
But the *Dhammapada* borrows such language to employ it in the service not
of gods, God, or an Absolute but of peace. This tactic of usurpation and conceptual redefinition of widely used terms is common in Buddhist literature,
and we will encounter many examples in what follows.

7–8. *sense faculties.* In some instances, these are given as five physical "powers" of
sense perception: eyes, ears, nose, tongue, and body (see, for instance, *Majjhimanikāya* 43.21), and in others, six, including mind, sometimes referred to
as an "internal," as opposed to "physical," faculty (see *Indriyabhāvanā Sutta*,
"The Development of the Faculties," *Majjhimanikāya* 152).

7. *Māra.* (See also note 37.) In ancient India, Māra was the personification of
death. Metaphorically, Māra is the force that pursues, tempts, and ultimately
destroys mortals. The word is, in fact, cognate with English words for death
and dying such as "mortality," "morbid," "murder," "mortal." The Buddha,
who persistently cautioned against reifying fluid, abstract principles—in
this case, positing a divine being behind a natural process—redefines the
term. In short, Māra is the grasping tendency of the psychological-physical
conglomerate, commonly referred to as a "self."

There is an entire *sutta* devoted to the Buddha's encounters with Māra. On
each occasion, Māra attempts to hinder the Buddha in some way. And each
time, the Buddha sees through his attempt, whereupon Māra disappears. In one
instance, Māra comes immediately after the Buddha attains full awakening.
The Buddha is reflecting on his previous path of austerity, which led him to
near starvation. He thinks, "It is good indeed that I am freed from that useless grueling asceticism!" Māra approaches him with these discouraging words.

> Having deviated from the austere practice
> by which men purify themselves,
> being impure, you think you are pure.
> You have missed the path to purity!

The Buddha understands that this is Māra speaking, or communicating to
him in some manner, and replies:

Having known as useless any austerity
aimed at the immortal state,
that all such penances are futile,
like oars and rudder on dry land,

by developing the path to awakening—
virtue, concentration, and wisdom—
I have attained supreme purity;
you are defeated, End-maker!

> (*Mārasaṃyutta*, "Connected Discourses with Māra,"
> *Saṃyuttanikāya* 1.4 [446-448])

It is interesting, of course, that Māra continues to harass the Buddha after his awakening. This might suggest that Māra is more than a mere metaphor for internal, psychological forces. Bhikkhu Bodhi, the eminent translator of the *Majjhimanikāya* and *Saṃyuttanikāya* believes this is the case. He writes, "It is evident that the thought world of the suttas does not conceive Māra only as a personification of humankind's moral frailty, but sees him as a real evil deity out to frustrate the efforts of those intent on winning the ultimate goal" (*The Connected Discourses of the Buddha: A Translation of the Saṃyutta Nikāya* [Boston: Wisdom Publications, 2000, p. 79).

I may be engaging in the further desacralization of the universe, or simple psychologizing, but it seems possible to me that Māra's continued pursuit of the Buddha suggests that awakening is not the überpious, super-human event that later defenders of the faith make it out to be (unlike Zen: remember the masters' characterization of *buddha* as "a dried shit stick"!). In any case, it is not difficult to see why scholars have called Māra names such as the Tempter, the Evil One, the Buddhist Satan, and the Destroyer.

8. *Living without an eye to pleasure.* This might also be understood in a narrower sense; namely, as a reference to a meditation technique known as "mindfulness of the body," in which the practitioner attempts to overcome attachment to his or her body by investigating its "foul" nature (see *Kāyagatāsati Sutta*, "Mindfulness of the Body," *Majjhimanikāya* 119). In this case, the translation could read "dwelling in the contemplation of foulness."

9–10. *stain.* In Pāli, there is a play on words here that cannot be replicated in translation: stain/yellow robe = *kasāva/kāsāva*. The yellow-stained robe refers to the clothing worn by Theravādan monks to this day.

11–12. *field of wrong intention, field of right intention.* A reference to the second component of the noble eightfold path, and its opposite. (See note 38. See also *Mahāsatipaṭṭhāna Sutta*, "The Great Discourse on the Foundations of Mindfulness," *Dīghanikāya* 22.21, for the formulaic enumeration of the eightfold path, and *Dvedhāvitakka Sutta,* "Two Kinds of Thought," *Majjhimanikāya* 19, for a discussion of *sammāsaṃkappa,* right intention or right thought.)

13–14. *mind.* Whereas the term for "mind" in verses 1 and 2 was *manas,* here it is *citta.* These two, plus a third term, *viññāṇa,* are often used synonymously in the Nikāyas to denote the human capacity for cognition and awareness. Each term does, however, have its particular uses. As we have seen, *manas* has several functions. It is the sixth sense faculty, having thoughts as its analogues to sounds, scents, et cetera; it "experiences the domain" of each of the other five, that is, it serves a coordinating role in perception; it, along with body and speech, is a vehicle for action (*kamma/karma*). We also saw that *viññāṇa,* or consciousness, is what occurs when a sense faculty has contact with its object. So, when the eye meets the visible object, eye-consciousness arises. Another usage of *viññāṇa* is to account for the apparent streamlike continuity through this and successive lives. Finally, *citta* seems to have the sense that we find in the *Yogasūtras* of Patañjali (ca. second century B.C.E.), namely, as the felt center of individual experience. (See B. K. S. Iyengar, *Light on the Yoga Sūtras of Patañjali* [London: Aquarian Press, 1993].)

For further reading on the concept of mind and consciousness in Buddhism, see Steven Collins, *Selfless Persons: Imagery and Thought in Theravāda Buddhism* (Cambridge: Cambridge University Press, 1982); Peter Harvey, *The Selfless Mind: Personality and Consciousness, and Nirvana in Early Buddhism* (Surrey: Curzon Press, 1995); and Dan Lusthaus, *Buddhist Phenomenology* (London: RoutledgeCurzon, 2003). For an overview of broader Indian philosophical conceptions of consciousness, see Bina Gupta, *Cit: Consciousness* (Oxford: Oxford University Press, 2003).

15–18. *in the world beyond.* Rebirth, or continued becoming (*punabbhava*), is an axiomatic, pan-Indian belief. It is axiomatic because it follows as a matter of consequence from two theories that are held to be self-evident. The first is *kamma/karma,* which, for Buddhists, states that all intentional bodily, verbal, and mental action (*kamma/karma* means "action"; cognate with Latin *caritas* [hard *c*] > English "charity") invariably generates consequences (*phala,* fruit). Just as different kinds of fruit vary in their gestation, growth, and ripening periods, so do actions. Many consequences are not borne out in a single span of life. (See *Mahākammavibhanga Sutta,* "The Greater Exposition of Action," *Majjhimanikāya* 136.)

This theory of action leads to the second Indian theory supporting the idea of continual rebirth and redeath, that of an eternally oscillating universe. In this view, fundamental to Indian cosmology, the universe undergoes an eternal cycle of emergence, evolution, and destruction, oscillating perpetually between expansion and contraction, activity and calm. At the moment of greatest stillness and unity, emergence and expansion begin; at the moment of greatest activity and multiplicity, calm and concord. (See Richard Davis, *Ritual in an Oscillating Universe* [Princeton: Princeton University Press, 1991], and Randy Kloetzli, *Buddhist Cosmology* [New Delhi: Motilal Banarsidass, 1983].) Where—when—in such a picture is there a place for *beginning* and *end*? The Buddha, in fact, considered ideas such as *beginning* and *end* to be based on erroneous, speculative, metaphysical views. (See *Brahmajāla Sutta,* "The Supreme Net," *Dīghanikāya* 1.1.30–2.22.)

In the Buddhist view, the capacity of consciousness to re-arise in this or another world after death is no more remarkable than its re-arising an hour from now in another room. That is, the process of life, death, rebirth, re-death, rebirth is occurring continually at different degrees of severity. While it is not difficult to observe the arising and passing of consciousness from moment to moment, since it is directly before us, seeing this process over greater spans of time and space requires meditative mastery. As this point suggests, however, Buddhists hold that it *is* possible to observe earlier "moments" in the beginningless stream of consciousness. The following description of meditative insight makes this point clear.

> When his concentrated mind is thus [i.e., through meditation] purified, bright, unblemished, rid of imperfection, malleable, wieldy, steady, and attained to imperturbability, [the meditator] directs it to knowledge of the recollection of past lives. He recollects his manifold past lives, that is, one birth, two births . . . a hundred births, a thousand births, a hundred thousand births, many aeons of world contraction and expansion. Thus, with their aspects and particulars he recollects his manifold past lives. . . . So, too, a [practitioner] recollects his manifold past lives.
>
> (*Majjhimanikāya* 39.19)

19–20. *share in the religious life.* Ideally, these verses might be understood by the present reader as a vital, fundamental prescription for reading. The difference between merely reading or reciting a text—the *Dhammapada,* for example!—and "practic[ing] accordingly" is the difference between being an ordinary, deluded person and becoming an accomplished (*arahant*), awakened (*buddha*) one.

CHAPTER TWO

DILIGENCE
अप्पमादवग्गो

Chapter One created a framework by introducing foundational Buddhist themes. This chapter begins to provide some of the fine points necessary for following the path. It does so by focusing on specific dispositions necessary for awakening to "the way things are." While the title indicates a quality of special significance, diligence, others are mentioned as well, such as energy, thoughtfulness, and restraint. Chapter Two can thus be seen as elaborating on the final two verses of Chapter One. It makes clear that habits of behavior, and one in particular, are absolutely necessary for "practic[ing] accordingly" and having "a share in the religious life." Again, this is quite commonsensical. Doesn't the acquisition of virtually any skill—from learning to hold a spoon as a baby to becoming a virtuoso musician—require habituated behavior and diligent effort? This is the idea behind "mastery," or the perfecting of particular skills.

A crucial question, of course, is, What skills are being perfected? Tyrants master skills, too. This chapter begins to lay out the skills required for a very specific type of person: a *buddha*, an awakened one. The trait of diligence is of such importance in the undertaking of the Buddhist path that, in his final words to his disciples, the dying Buddha said, "All conditioned things are subject to decay; strive with diligence!" (*Mahāparinibbāna Sutta,* "The Buddha's Last Days," *Dīghanikāya* 16.6.7).

NOTES

21. *Diligence.* The lexical range of the term that I am translating as "diligence" (*appamāda*) includes "thoughtfulness," "carefulness," "conscientiousness," "watchfulness," "vigilance," "earnestness," "zeal."

21. *the deathless.* This is one of several metaphorical terms for the final goal of the Buddhist path, known as *nibbāna/nirvāṇa* (see note 23). In the Vedas (dating from ca. 1500 B.C.E.), the basis for the dominant religion in India at the time of the Buddha, immortality, or the deathless (*amata/amṛta,* stemming from the root *mṛ,* from which is derived the English "mortality") was the sought-after ultimate condition. There, it meant roughly what it does in its English usage: existence of a permanent identity in a perpetual state of vitality.

In the Buddhist usage, however, it means something quite different. In brief, the deathless is a "state" or "condition" (these terms are, of course, really just additional metaphors) that is without death because it is also without birth, arising, or production. That is, because of the mindful and nongrasping comportment of the individual toward the phenomenal world, it is not the case that a given phenomenon has even been "born." In one passage, the Buddha expresses this fact as follows:

> [Practitioners], dwell with your minds well established in the four establishments of mindfulness. Do not let the Deathless be lost on you. In what four? Here a [practitioner] dwells contemplating the body in the body, ardent, clearly comprehending, mindful, having removed covetousness and displeasure in regard to the world. He dwells contemplating feelings in feelings . . . mind in mind . . . phenomena in phenomena. . . . Dwell, [practitioners], with your mind well established in these four establishments of mindfulness. Do not let the Deathless be lost on you. (*Satipaṭṭhāna-saṃyutta,* "Connected Discourses on the Establishment of Mindfulness," *Saṃyuttanikāya* 5.47.41)

The "establishment of mindfulness" (*satipaṭṭhāna*) is a central practice in Buddhism (see *Satipaṭṭhāna Sutta,* "The Foundations of Mindfulness," *Majjhimanikāya* 10). Mindfulness (*sati*) is related to *the all* and to the *proper range* discussed above in that its founding or setting up (*paṭṭhāna*) establishes precisely the proper frame of reference for living one's life in its all, in its fullness, at the very instant that it transpires—now. The Buddhist method for becoming skilled at living life as it actually occurs is just this practice of mindfulness.

Mindfulness and "the deathless" relate to each other in the following manner. Imagine that the feeling of anger wells up inside you. By applying attentiveness to that welling up, that is, by being ardent, clearly comprehending, and mindful toward the anger, being neither attracted nor averse to it, you are able to alter fundamentally the nature of that anger. It is converted from an all-consuming wave that constitutes your entire identity at that moment to an object of calm observation. With the practice of mindfulness, the anger, as a powerful, identity-consuming force, might be transformed into more constructive emotions, or dissolved outright. The Buddha considered this such a potent practice that he called it the "direct" or even "only" path. (The Pāli term, *ekāyano maggo,* may be understood in either way; see Bhikkhu Bodhi's comment in *The Middle Length Discourses of the Buddha: A Translation of the Majjhima Nikāya* [1995; Boston: Wisdom Publications, 2001], p. 1188, n. 135.)

> [Practitioners], this is the direct path for the purification of beings, for the surmounting of sorrow and lamentation, for the disappearance of pain and grief, for the attainment of the true way, for the realization of Nibbāna—namely the four foundations of mindfulness. (*Satipaṭṭhāna Sutta,* "The Foundations of Mindfulness," *Majjhimanikāya* 10.2)

22. *pasture of the noble ones.* The teachings, practices, et cetera (pasture) that constitute people as accomplished (*arahant*) and awakened (*buddha*), in other words, noble ones.

23. *unbinding.* The goal of the Buddhist path. I am following Thanissaro Bhikkhu in translating *nibbāna/nirvāṇa* as "unbinding." The term *nirvāṇa* (this is the more common, Sanskrit, spelling) has found its way, via the Beats, the hippies, grunge, punk, New Age, and Madison Avenue, into everyday English usage. The common, and not incorrect, understanding of *nirvāṇa* is that it concerns an extinguishing, or blowing out of a flame. This is also how it is routinely rendered in secondary works on Buddhism, as well as in translations of the primary literature. For those readers who have the patience of the slow, and wish to wade through the etymological and philological intricacies of the verbal formation (prefix) *nir* + (root) *vā,* I recommend Steven Collins's extraordinary *Nirvana and Other Buddhist Felicities: Utopias of the Pali Imaginaire* (Cambridge: Cambridge University Press, 1998), particularly pages 191–203.

So, "blowing out" is only one way of construing the term. Another way that Buddhists themselves have understood the meaning of *nibbāna/nirvāṇa* is precisely as "unbinding." Since I am following Thanissaro Bhikkhu's lead, I will let him speak for himself in defending this unusual choice. I am quoting him at such length because I think his argument is an important one. It serves as a gentle nudge away from what has become an ingrained habit of Buddhist-English translation. Also, doing so will go some way toward explaining what *nibbāna/nirvāṇa* "is."

The Buddha's choice of the word Unbinding (*nibbāna*)—which literally means the extinguishing of a fire—derives from the way that the physics of fire was viewed at his time. As fire burned, it was seen as clinging to its fuel in a state of entrapment and agitation. When it went out, it let go of its fuel, growing calm and free. Thus, when the Indians of his time saw a fire going out, they did not feel that they were watching extinction. Rather, they were seeing a metaphorical lesson in how freedom could be attained by letting go.   (*The Wings of Awakening* [Barre, Mass.: Dhamma Dana Publications, 1996], p. 6)

[Now quoting a canonical passage; the Buddha said,] if a [practitioner] abandons passion for the property of form . . . feeling . . . perception . . . mental processes . . . consciousness, then owing to the abandoning of passion, the support is cut off, and there is no base for consciousness. Consciousness, thus unestablished, not proliferating, not performing any function, is released. Owing to its release, it stands still. Owing to its stillness, it is contented. Owing to its contentment, it is not agitated. Not agitated, [the practitioner] is totally "nibbāna-ized" right within. (*Samyuttanikāya* 3.22.53)

[Thanissaro Bhikkhu again.] This being the set of events—stillness, independence, unattachment—associated with the extinguishing of fire and the attainment of the goal, it would appear that, of all the etymologies offered to explain the word "nibbāna," the closest one to its original connotation is that quoted by Buddhaghosa in *The Path of Purification* (8.247) [a premier authoritative source for the Theravāda; fifth century C.E.]. There, he derives the word from the negative prefix *nir* plus *vāna*, or binding: Unbinding.

Modern scholars have tended to scorn this derivation as fanciful, and they favor such hypotheses as "blowing out" (etc.). But although these hypotheses might make sense in terms of modern Western ideas about fire, they are hardly relevant to the way nibbāna is used in the Canon. Freedom, on the other hand, is more than relevant. It is central, both in the context of ancient Indian theories of fire and in the psychological context of attaining the goal: "Not agitated, [the practitioner] is totally unbound right within." . . . What kind of unbinding? We have already gained some kind of idea—liberation from dependency and limitations, from agitation and death. (*The Mind Like Fire Unbound* [Barre, Mass.: Dhamma Dana Publications, 1996], pp. 41–42)

Now, I am taking one small step further than Thanissaro Bhikkhu suggests by writing "unbinding," with a lowercase *u*. First of all, the value of translating *nibbāna/nirvāṇa* at all—it is often left untranslated—is that doing so de-exoticizes what is held by Buddhists to be an utterly human process. But "Unbinding" creates the danger of reification, that is, the danger that some readers will turn this process into a static place or thing, like the Absolute, the Transcendent, God, et cetera. To do so would be to misunderstand the entirety of the Buddha's teaching.

27. *Meditating.* The classic, ancient Indian work on spiritual practice, Patañjali's *Yogasūtras* (see note 13–14), gives this succinct definition of meditation: "Meditation is stilling the fluctuations in consciousness" (*sūtra* 1.2). The term for meditation there is *yoga,* one of several employed by the earliest Buddhist traditions, along with *jhāya* (the term used in this *Dhammapada* verse; it is cognate with the more familiar Sanskrit *dhyāna,* which becomes Chinese *ch'an,* Korean *son,* and Japanese *zen*).

The basic form of meditation recommended by the Buddha is called *ānāpānasati,* mindfulness of breathing or, technically, "mindfulness of [or with, by means of, or through] inhalation and exhalation." In the discourse by this name (*Majjhimanikāya* 118), the Buddha gives instructions for this basic meditation.

> [Practitioners], when mindfulness of breathing is developed and cultivated, it is of great fruit and great benefit. When mindfulness of breathing is developed and cultivated, it fulfills the four foundations of mindfulness [see note 21, "*the deathless*"]. When the four foundations of mindfulness are developed and cultivated, they fulfill the seven awakening factors [dispositions necessary for awakening: mindfulness, investigation, persistence, rapture, serenity, concentration, equanimity]. When the seven awakening factors are developed and cultivated, they fulfill true knowledge and deliverance.
>
> And how, [practitioners], is mindfulness of breathing developed and cultivated, so that it is of great fruit and great benefit?
>
> Here a [practitioner], gone to the forest or to the root of a tree or to an empty hut, sits down; having folded his legs crosswise, set his body straight, and established mindfulness in front of him, ever mindful he breathes in, mindful he breathes out.
>
> Breathing in long, he understands: "I breathe in long"; or breathing out long, he understands: "I breathe out long." Breathing in short, he understands: "I breathe in short"; or breathing out short, he understands: "I breathe out short." He trains thus: "I will breathe in experiencing the whole body [of breath]"; he trains thus: "I will breathe out experiencing the whole body [of breath]." He trains thus: "I will breathe in tranquillizing the bodily formation"; he trains thus: "I will breathe out tranquil-

lizing the bodily formation." (*Ānāpānasati Sutta,* "Mindfulness of Breathing," *Majjhimanikāya* 118.15–18)

28. *palace of wisdom.* See note 38.
30. *Maghavan.* Meaning "bountiful," this is an epithet for the Vedic god Indra, ruler of the atmosphere and sky. Early scholars of comparative mythology saw Indra as the "Indian Jupiter."
30. *radiant ones.* This is a translation of the Pāli and Sanskrit word *deva.* It is routinely translated as "god." Deriving from the verbal root *div,* it is cognate with the English "divine," "deity," "day," and "diva." And, like the last two terms in particular, *deva* refers to a dazzling, brilliant, resplendent appearance. For this reason, "god," as a synonym for "deity," is not incorrect; but, given Western and theistic conceptions of god/God, it *does* create unnecessary problems. In ancient India, as attested in the Vedas, the natural world, consisting of earthly, atmospheric, and sky realms, was held to be permeated by such vivid appearances, manifesting as wind, fire, sound, speech, thunder, and so on.

The cosmology assumed by the Buddha preserved the notion of a triple world but divided it into the sense-sphere realm (*kāmadhātu*), the form realm (*rūpadhātu*), and the formless realm (*arūpadhātu*). The first is populated by beings who are driven primarily by sense desire (hence that name). These are further divided into eleven spheres, or destinations (*gati*). The first four are "bad" or unfortunate (*duggati*) realms of existence (the "lower worlds," routinely translated as "hells"), animal realm, ghost realm, violent "demigod" (*asura*) realm. The human realm is the fifth possible place of birth/rebirth. The remaining six realms of the *kāmadhātu* are populated by *devas.* These, and the human realm, are considered "good" or fortunate destinations (*sugati*).

In the *rūpadhātu,* form realm, the material properties of beings have become extremely subtle. The beings who are born here experience existence through meditative, rather than sensual, contact. These realms, subdivided into sixteen spheres, are populated exclusively by classes of *devas* with names such as "measureless radiance," "streaming radiance," and "steady aura." Each of the *rūpadhātu* realms, in addition to being an actual "world" or place of existence held to be as real as our human world, is accessible to meditative absorption (the four *jhānas*) by humans (called, for example, "serene realm," "beautiful realm," "clear-sighted realm"). The top five of these, called "pure abodes," are, in fact, accessible *only* to advanced meditators as a rebirth possibility.

Finally, the formless realm, *arūpadhātu,* consists of four spheres of such exquisiteness that they cannot be spoken of as "places" at all. The beings of these realms exist in mentality only, without a physical basis. The names of these spheres will give the reader some indication of their nature: "base of infinity of space," "base of infinity of consciousness," "base of nothingness," "base of neither-perception-nor-nonperception." These, too, are accessible from our human world via meditative absorptions. For this reason, the Buddha did not consider this "map" of the universe theoretical: the entire cosmos, in its manifold dimensions, is knowable.

A crucial point to bear in mind concerning the Buddhist cosmology is that every being in each of the three realms is subject to pain, suffering, and repeated births and deaths. Thus, even the "gods" are mortal. It is true that their lives are, by human standards, inconceivably long and pleasurable, but they do end, and the gods will eventually experience pain (*dukkha*) again, as the following dialogue indicates. (See also note 15–18.)

> [A great king asks the Buddha:] "Venerable sir, how is it: are there gods?"
> "Why do you ask that, great king?"
> "Venerable sir, I was asking whether those gods come back to this [human] state or whether they do not."
> "Great king, those gods who are still subject to afflictions come back to this [human] state, those gods who are no longer subject to afflictions do not come back to this [human] state." (*Majjhimanikāya* 90.13; on the possibility of being reborn in a *deva* realm, see 41.18–42)

31. *practitioner.* As explained in the Introduction, my wish to have this translation speak to contemporary readers, whether they consider themselves Buddhist or not, governs my decision to translate terms for monastic and ascetic figures simply as "practitioner." Here, the Pāli reads *bhikkhu*, meaning "mendicant" in the earliest days of Buddhism, and later "monk." It comes from a verbal root for "begging," hence, one who begs alms. (See note 266.)

31. *every fetter, coarse and subtle.* There are ten fetters. Each of the four stages of the path—stream-entry, once-returner, non-returner, and *arahant*—is defined in part by the fetters that are thrown off by the practitioner. Five are coarse or "lower": (1) belief in an abiding personality; (2) doubt in the teachings; (3) misplaced confidence in the ability of rituals to lead to awakening; (4) attachment to sensuality; and (5) ill will toward others. Five are subtle or "higher": (6) craving for the world of form; (7) craving for the formless world; (8) conceit; (9) restlessness; and (10) ignorance. (See *Dīghanikāya* 33.2.1 [7–8].)

─༄༅─

CHAPTER THREE

MIND
चित्तवग्गो

The word translated as "mind" in this chapter is *citta,* the sense of personal identity and the "center" of lived experience. *Citta* is the human capacity to attend to things, to think, plan, scheme, be anxious, ponder, and long. This is a range of function that includes cognitive and affective, as well as reflective, qualities. For this reason, *citta* is often translated as "heart," or even "heart-mind." In light of the work that it does, *citta* seems to come closest to our colloquial use of "ego" (although the notion of the *ahamkāra,* "I-maker," might be a nearer equivalent).

In any case, the Buddha saw *citta* as the prime culprit in the pain of existence.

> By what is the world led around?
> By what is it dragged here and there?
> What is the one thing that has
> all under its control?
>
> The world is led around by mind [*citta*].
> By mind it is led here and there.
> Mind is the one thing that has
> all under its control.
>
> (*Saṃyuttanikāya* 1.1.205, 206)

So, if a person is to live a life of well-being, it is *citta* that must be calmed. The central theme of this chapter is therefore the restraint, taming, and guarding of the mind. To support the case for achieving this restraint, the chapter also indicates the nature of the mind, as well as the consequences of *not* taming the mind.

NOTES

33. *mind.* On *citta,* see note 13.

34. *death.* This is Māra. (See notes 7 and 37.)

35–36. *ease.* This is a translation of *sukha,* the analogue to *dukkha* (pain, unease). See the introduction to Chapter Fifteen.

37. *bonds of Māra.* (See also note 7.) In the story of the Buddha's awakening, cobbled together from several canonical passages and elaborated on in the first-century C.E. poem by Aśvaghoṣa, *Buddhacārita,* "The Life of the Buddha," Māra attempts to hinder the soon-to-be-Buddha (in some versions, this hindrance extends to the first moments of the awakening) in his quest for liberation. One way of understanding liberation is to see it as a release from the means through which Māra binds us: craving, discontent, and passion. Māra's three daughters came to the Buddha to destroy his concentration and derail his endeavor. They came—

> glittering with beauty—
> Taṇha, Arati, and Rāga [Craving, Discontent, and Passion]—
> But the teacher swept them away right there
> as the wind, a fallen cotton tuft.
>
> (*Mārasaṃyutta,* "Connected Discourses with Māra,"
> *Saṃyuttanikāya* 1.4 [518])

Recall, too, that Māra "gains an opening, gains a foothold" when we wander outside "our proper domain, our ancestral home" (i.e., when we fall short in the practices of mindfulness, meditative calm, et cetera). (See note 1–2, "*pain . . . ease.*")

38. *insightful knowledge.* This is the important Buddhist category *paññā/prajñā.* The verbal formation, (prefix) *pa* + (root) *jan,* from which it is derived (Sanskrit *pra* + *jñā*), has a wide lexical range. The primary meaning is "to know." But the term is used additionally to denote mental activities that concern more or less what we in the modern West consider the domain of the "intellect": to perceive, understand, comprehend, recognize, investigate, consider, ascertain.

As early as the Upaniṣads (ca. 900-300 B.C.E.), *jñāna* began to be used in a technical sense to denote a special kind or quality of knowledge, one that is derived from meditative insight. It came to mean "higher knowledge." The term is thus often translated as "wisdom." In the Upaniṣads, higher knowledge or wisdom consisted in the direct and thorough realization of the unity of the individual self, *ātman*, and the universal substance, *brahman*. For the Buddha, of course, higher knowledge, wisdom, meant something quite different. In the threefold division of the eightfold path as morality (*sīla*: right speech, action, and livelihood), concentration (*samādhi*: right mindfulness, right concentration, or meditation), and wisdom (*paññā*), wisdom, the third subdivision, consists of right view (*sammādiṭṭhi*) and right thought (or intention) (*sammāsaṃkappa*) (see note 191). The Buddha explains his understanding of "wisdom" as follows.

> And what, [practitioners], is Right View? It is the knowledge of pain (*dukkha*), the knowledge of the origin of pain, the knowledge of the cessation of pain, the knowledge of the way of practice leading to the cessation of pain.
> And what, [practitioners], is Right Thought? The thought of renunciation, the thought of non-ill-will, the thought of harmlessness. This is called Right Thought. (*Mahāsatipaṭṭhāna Sutta*, "The Greater Discourse on the Foundations of Mindfulness," *Dīghanikāya* 22.21)

This is, of course, a shorthand version of the entire edifice of Buddhist doctrine and practice. For example, "the knowledge of the origin of pain," that is, the first noble truth, requires insight into the structure and processes of what we call "the person"; "the knowledge of the cessation of pain," the second noble truth, requires insight into the nature of craving, and so on. (See *Dhammacakkappavattana Sutta*, "The Discourse Setting in Motion the Wheel of the Doctrine," *Saṃyuttanikāya* 5.56.11. This *sutta* is considered by Buddhists to be the first teaching given by the newly awakened Buddha.)

So, it should be clear that the important point is to *thoroughly realize* or gain *insight into* the nature of *dukkha*—pain, unease, dissatisfaction, suffering. The English word "knowledge" does not convey this notion strongly enough, and "wisdom" is too vague (although I do render it thus in several later instances where such vagueness seems to be in order).

39. *moistened by passion*. The term for "moistened," *avassuta*, is derived from the same root as *āsava*. (See note 89, "*impulses.*")

41. *consciousness*. Along with the other two terms that we have seen concerning the mental faculty, *manas* and *citta*, *viññāṇa*, "consciousness," constitutes the core of the Buddhist understanding of "mind." (See notes 1–2, "*preceded by mind are phenomena*," and, for further references, 13–14.)

CHAPTER FOUR

FLOWERS

पुप्फवग्गो

Flowers have an ambivalent value for a tradition that is simultaneously wary and deeply appreciative of the alluring, shimmering mirage that is the world. Death will seize and carry away the person who gathers flowers *only*. But the person who is skillful in extracting nourishing nectar from the world, like a bee gently drinking from a flower, leaving the petals unharmed, will derive great benefit from that very same object. This ambiguity points to the central Buddhist theme of void or emptiness (*suññatā*), symbolically alluded to in this chapter. Value, meaning, significance, and so on, do not inhere in the objects that constitute one's world. They have, rather, the quality of a mirage, whose specific appearance depends on what the perceiver of the mirage makes of the display of heat and light before him or her.

A flower (the world) is, indeed, by nature beautiful and enticing; and one may derive great pleasure from its scent and bloom. There is, however, one serious limit to its ability to ensure happiness: its scent never flows against the wind. That is, the nature of its pleasure goes in one direction only—toward the dissolution and destruction that is endemic to the natural world. The power of acquired Buddhist dispositions, by contrast, does flow against the wind, diffusing real joy in all directions. It is ironic that Buddhism is popularly viewed as a religion that encourages us to "go with the flow" if we would attain some measure of happiness and well-being. On the contrary, the Buddha repeatedly said of himself that he is one who goes *against* the flow, against the current, of the world. Only such a person may acquire the virtues capable of "wafting supreme" throughout the world. There is, however, no suggestion here of a turning *away* from the world. The final verse of the chapter makes sure of this when it says that it is precisely in the midst of the world that a lotus of perfumed fragrance is born, grows, and shines.

NOTES

44. *death.* Here, this translates Yama, the Lord of Death in Indian cosmology, who governs the realms of the lower worlds. (See note 30, "*radiant ones.*" See in addition *Majjhimanikāya* 3.130 and *Aṅguttaranikāya* 1.138–142.)

44. *verse on the way.* As in the title of this book, this translates *dhammapada*. (See Introduction.)

45. *seeker.* Together with *samaṇa* (see notes 31, "*practitioner,*" 141–142, and 265), I translate *sekha* as "seeker." The Pāli term *sekha* (from the Sanskrit verbal root *śikṣ* "to learn"), however, has the important technical meaning of "trainee," specifically, one who has reached one of the three "streams" but is not yet an accomplished *arahant.* For canonical references on the "three streams" (stream-enterer, once-returner, and non-returner), see Bhikkhu Bodhi, *The Middle Length Discourses of the Buddha: A Translation of the Majjhima Nikāya* (1995; Boston: Wisdom Publications, 2001), pp. 41–43. See also note 178. For a full description of the trainee requirements of a *sekha,* see *Sekha Sutta,* "The Disciple in Higher Training," *Majjhimanikāya* 53. In brief, the training consists of mastering fifteen modes of conduct (e.g., guarding of the doors of the sense faculties, moderation in eating), and three types of knowledge (e.g., recollection of manifold past lives).

46. *as foam . . . as a shimmering mirage.* These are instructive similes regarding the Buddhist views on the nonsubstantial (*anattā*) and impermanent (*anicca*) nature of the phenomenal world. It is not accurate to say that a mirage *does not* exist. The person who sees a mirage sees *something.* And in that seeing, real emotions, responses, and consequences are effected. But, as common sense tells us, it is also not accurate to say that a mirage *does* exist. A mirage is just an illusion caused by light reflecting through several layers of air of varying temperatures. These external conditions combine with internal, subjective ones to fashion the particular image that is "seen": the parched desert traveler sees a lush oasis. His fellow traveler, however, sees something different, or nothing at all. Why? Because he experiences a different confluence of external and internal conditions. (Think of the symbolism of the etymologically related word "mirror.")

What makes this malleability of "reality" possible is precisely the fact that there is nothing supporting it beyond these ever-arising, ever-falling, ever-changing conditions. So, for Buddhists, all of the phenomenal world is like a mirage: it appears, but nothing stands underneath it (i.e., it is literally *nonsubstantial*). This nonsubstantiality is verified every time you see, hear, taste, et cetera, something different from your friend, who is seeing, hearing, tasting that very "same" painting, song, or cookie. (Later Buddhists had a saying that captured this miragelike nature of the world: Things are not as they appear; nor are they otherwise.)

While the early Buddhism reflected in the Pāli canonical literature usually applies such similes to the body and the person, later Buddhists would apply them more directly to an analysis of reality. The primary conceptual tool used for this analytical work was *śūnyatā*, "void" or "emptiness." There is a common misunderstanding that both this term and this type of analysis are Mahāyāna innovations. In fact, they lay at the heart of the Buddha's teaching from the outset.

49. *As a bee . . . does not harm.* An instructive simile on the Buddhist virtue of *ahiṃsa*, gentleness or nonharm in body, speech, and mind.

54. *excellent person.* This term refers to the model for the ideal layperson. The Pāli word, *sappurisa*, means "good, true, superior, or excellent person." A brief definition runs as follows:

> When a person supports his parents,
> and respects the family elders;
> when his speech is gentle and courteous,
> and he refrains from divisive words;
> when he strives to remove meanness,
> is truthful, and vanquishes anger,
> the radiant ones call him
> truly a superior [an excellent] person.
>
> (*Saṃyuttanikāya* 1.11.11[1])

This definition emphasizes the mastery of ethical behavior (*sīla*) and generosity (*cāga*). Other statements about the *sappurisa* intone the qualities of faith (*saddhā*) and insight or wisdom (*paññā*). The following statement shows, in addition, that it is following the eightfold path that constitutes "excellence" in a person, and that this path was open to the laity.

> And what, [practitioners], is the superior [excellent] person? Here someone is of right view, right intention, right speech, right action, right livelihood, right effort, right mindfulness, right concentration. This is called the superior person. (*Saṃyuttanikāya* 5.45.25[5])

See, further, Nyanaponika Thera and Bhikkhu Bodhi, *Numerical Discourses of the Buddha: An Anthology of Suttas from the Aṅguttara Nikāya* (Walnut Creek, Calif.: AltaMira Press, 1999), pp. 23-24. For a full description of the Buddha's advice to the laity, see *Dīghanikāya* 31.

58–59. *lotus.* The lotus flower becomes a widespread metaphor for the *bodhisattva* in Mahāyāna Buddhism. In fact, a major impetus in the development of this new Buddhist ideal—replacing that of the *arahant*—was the perceived need to move away from the ascetic impulses of Buddhism and toward restructured, streamlined, lay-driven ones. It is interesting that, as with much of Mahāyāna and even Vajrayāna, the seeds of those innovations lay in the old *suttas.* For example, like the *bodhisattva,* who is characterized by his or her abiding compassion for, and repeated participation in, the world, the Buddha exhorts the practitioner to dwell "trembling for the welfare of all living beings" (*Sāmaññaphala Sutta,* "The Fruits of the Homeless Life," *Dīghanikāya* 2.43–62).

CHAPTER FIVE

THE CHILDISH PERSON
बालवग्गो

One way of going through life is as a perpetual child. In religious traditions that emphasize faith in an external, omnipotent being, this approach is usually viewed as not only constructive but necessary. Childlike qualities such as acceptance, innocence, wonder, and subservience to authority are highly valued in theistic traditions. In Buddhism, a tradition that places emphasis on the personal development of specific skills—skills that form an individual into an "accomplished" or "awakened" one—a completely different view is held. A childish person who is actually an adult suffers from, and is limited by, childish traits, such as unripe experience, poor judgment, uninformed decision making, hasty action, weak self-control, and so on. The first set of childlike qualities mentioned above are considered by Buddhists to be constructive only when they are *skillfully* applied; otherwise, they will hamper growth. A person who can apply these traits in such a constructive manner is, of course, well on his or her way to emerging from childishness into skillfulness. This chapter, in fact, explicates only the first of three possible ways a person may behave in life. It and the two chapters that follow give a rough progressive typology of human beings: childish, skillful, and accomplished.

The sense of childishness in this chapter, however, is not restricted to the most obvious forms of behavior associated with that term. A person who ambitiously pursues material fortune, being pushed along by an ever-strengthening current of "I, me, and mine" is childish. So is one who acts as "an enemy" to himself because he lacks the skills necessary for achieving his aims. What percentage of humankind is included in these examples? A glance at today's newspaper will prove the point made in this chapter: we live collectively as lost, bewildered, wailing children.

NOTES

60. *round of birth and death.* This translates *saṃsāra*, a pan-Indian religious-cosmological concept that, along with *nibbāna / nirvāṇa*, becomes a foundational theme in Buddhism. Derived from the verbal formation (prefix) *saṃ* + (root) *sṛ*, it denotes flowing, wandering, roaming, passing through. In the Upaniṣads, where we find an early, pre-Buddhist expression of the view that continued existence or rebirth is undesirable, the connotation of *saṃsāra* as transmigration of a soul or self from life to life becomes normative.

   Buddhists, of course, reject the possibility of there being any actual entity or substance that transmigrates from moment to moment, much less from life to life (see note 62). The "person" is really just the continual arising and passing away of the "five aggregates" (*khandha*), which give the *appearance* of constituting an abiding self, soul, person, or identity. One canonical verse expresses the nature of the aggregates in vivid imagery.

> Form is like a lump of foam,
> feeling like a water bubble;
> perception is like a mirage,
> volitions [formations, fabrications]
> like a plantain tree
> [i.e., they consist of endless layers,
> like an onion, with, finally, no core],
> and consciousness like an illusion.
>
> However one may ponder it
> and carefully investigate it,
> it appears hollow and void
> when one views it carefully.
>
> (*Saṃyuttanikāya* 3.22.95)

The "round of birth and death," then, may be taken to signify: (1) the continuous, moment-to-moment flux of our lives, in the process of which there is an erroneous sense of an "I" who persists; and (2) the large-scale cycle of birth, aging, illness, and death (and rebirth) perpetuated by this error.

Note 30, "*radiant ones*," describes the realms of birth that, taken as a whole, constitute the "place" of *saṃsāra*. But it should be borne in mind that *saṃsāra* and *nibbāna/nirvāṇa* are as much psychological and epistemological terms as they are "spatial." In a system where space, time, and subjective experience are inseparable categories, is there really a difference? So, in the simplest terms, we can understand them as a matter of (1) ignorance of (a *saṃsāra*-ic view) or penetrative insight into (a *nibbāna/nirvāṇa*-ic view) the changing, nonsubstantial, painful nature of the phenomenal world; and (2) infatuation with (*saṃsāra*) or ending of (*nibbāna/nirvāṇa*) the three "poisons" of human existence—passion, aversion, and delusion.

60. *childish people.* This translates *bāla*, the same word in the title of the chapter. The common rendering of this word is "fool." While this is not incorrect, it is not very helpful. What exactly does "fool" signify? The primary meaning of *bāla* is in fact "childish," in the sense of both "young, not grown up" and "immature, puerile." While children (and adults who act like them) may do things that are, in the light of our mature wisdom, foolish, that does not make them "fools."

62. *not even a self.* The claim of nonself, *anattā*, is of such vital importance to Buddhism that many consider it to be Buddhism's very lifeblood. The claim holds that on a careful, detailed, and honest investigation of entities both inanimate and sentient (including, most importantly, oneself), there is nowhere to be found anything resembling the kind of existence that we commonly refer to as an "essence," "self," "soul," or "person."

It is not difficult to see this lack of essence in relation to an inanimate object. There is no need to posit an essential "carhood" dwelling within a collection of parts in order for us meaningfully to designate that object "car." A car is observably *just* this collection of parts, together with the accepted designation "car." Of course, there is no stability in this collection of parts. Parts wear out and are replaced. At some point, the entire "car" may have been replaced, so that nothing is left of the original one. This is, of course, in itself evidence of no inhering, permanent "carhood."

At a deeper structural level, physicists will tell us, not only is the car changing before our very eyes but what we see is really not even there. That is, because the trillions of atomic particles that constitute the physical form of the object are rising, interacting, transforming, and falling at such rapid, violent rates, the humming, vibrating, evanescent field of energy before us appears to be consistent and stable. This point shows the close relationship between *anattā* and the temporal feature of *anicca*, impermanence. It is precisely the lack of an abiding essence in things that makes possible the (observable) flux of the world. In fact, these two, together with *dukkha* (pain, dissatisfaction), make up what the Buddha called the three marks of existence (*tilakkhaṇa*), that is, the three qualities that determine the nature of *all* compounded objects (like the car, made up of parts), from a subatomic particle to the orb of the earth, from a fleeting thought to the very cosmos.

Now, none of this is terribly objectionable when the object of investigation is something like a car. But when a person turns this analysis to his or her own sense of selfhood, it becomes intolerable or, at best, unacceptable. The reason for this discomfort, according to Buddhism, is that the sense of a permanent, stable personal identity is the emotional and psychological bedrock of our existence. Indeed, for those who believe in a divinely created "soul" and an eternal afterlife for a permanent identity in an everlasting heaven in the presence of an unchanging God, *anattā* represents a threat to what they conceive to be the firmest imaginable foundation of security. It is in light of people's refusal to penetrate, much less accept, the three marks of existence that the Buddha had repeatedly to "teach it, make it known, explain it." Why is it of such importance to Buddhism to "ponder" this claim "and carefully investigate it"? Because, first of all, the view of self is founded on an error of misperception, and, second, this error is the source of unceasing grief, struggle, anxiety, and pain.

What is discovered in an honest investigation of the matter is that instead of a stable, integral self or identity—the persistent feeling of "I, me, mine"—there is a continual unfolding of a process consisting of five basic components, physical and psychological in nature. These are the *khandhas/skandhas*, the "heaps" or "aggregates" that account for the sense of there being a "person" undergoing the experiences of seeing, hearing, smelling, and so on. In brief, the five *khandhas* (translated in verses 202 and 374 as "aggregates") are as follows:

- Materiality (*rūpa*), the "givenness" of matter, which consists of the four elements: earth, water, fire, and air. In terms of the "person," this is the body.
- Sensation (*vedanā*), the feeling that arises when a sense faculty comes into contact with a sense object. For example, when the nose meets a scent, three sensations are possible: the scent may be experienced as pleasant, unpleasant, or neutral.
- Perception (*saññā*), the awareness of the object of sense. Given the form of an object "out there," and the contact between that form and a sense faculty, the object becomes discernible as a particular kind of object—one of sight, sound, scent, et cetera—within a field of awareness.
- Fabrication or fashioning (*saṅkhāra*), the closer discernment concerning the (perceived) qualities of the object. The important point here is that this discernment is based on personal proclivities, which in turn are products of conditioning (via family, culture, personal *karma*). This term is often translated as

"volition" since it is understood as an exercise of the will over the object being perceived to fashion it in a particular way. But the Sanskrit verbal formation from which the Pāli is derived, (prefix) *saṃ* + (root) *kṛ,* simply denotes "putting together, forming, embellishing." In the Buddhist view, this is precisely what we do whenever we see, hear, smell, taste, feel, or cognize an object. Every instance of seeing, et cetera, is an instance of "seeing as," the "as" deriving from our side, not from the side of the object.

· Consciousness (*viññāṇa*), the full awareness of the eye-object "in" the eye, of the ear-object "in" the ear, et cetera. It is important to note that consciousness is understood here as being focused through a particular mode of perception, and not as some kind of pervasive, ghostlike awareness. (See *Saṃyuttanikāya* 3.22.36.)

It is, then, the continual, rapid unfolding of this process that produces the sense of a person or self. And it is precisely this that is discovered when a person "ponders and carefully investigates" the matter. Since this is the mode of being in which humans are unavoidably involved, there is no notion in Buddhism of this process being some kind of evil or even problematic situation. The problem arises only when *clinging* by means of the *khandhas* is attempted, for the attempt to cling will always amount to a painful failure.

66–67. *detrimental actions . . . fruit.* The term *pāpa* is routinely translated with words that I find unhelpfully moralistic, such as "bad," "wrong," "evil," even "sin." Again, these are not incorrect renderings of *pāpa* (except for "sin"!). But as with *bāla* (see note 60, "*childish people*") as "fool," I am only left wondering what precisely "bad" is supposed to designate within the scope of Buddhism. These two verses are quite specific in this regard. An action is bad or wrong if it "bear[s] bitter fruit" and is "regret[ted]." The emphasis is thus on the subjective, rather than the legalistic, aspect of actions and their results. If, *for the person,* an action has results that are cause *for that person's* regret, then that action is detrimental *to that person.* This translation is also more consistent with the Buddha's insistence that harmful, detrimental forms of behavior can be skillfully "abandoned," and beneficial ones can be strengthened and developed.

It should be noted here as well that the term for "fruit" in verse 67, *vipāka* (to ripen, bear fruit, produce a result) is commonly, and inaccurately, substituted by the term *karma* (Pāli *kamma*) in contemporary North American Buddhist discourse. As these verses indicate, *kamma/karma* is the action, and *vipāka* is the result.

68. *beneficial.* My reasoning for translating *sādhu* here as "beneficial" rather than "good," is the same as that for *pāpa* as "detrimental," above.

70. *a blade of grass.* This is a reference to strict ascetic practice.

74. *the wanderer.* This translates *pabbajita*, "one who has gone forth." A *pabbajjā* is a novice practitioner who has left the domain of the home and society and, in the Buddha's day, wandered around, begging alms for sustenance and undergoing training in the teaching.

75. *practitioner.* This translates *bhikkhu.* (See note 31, "*practitioner.*")

CHAPTER SIX

THE SKILLED PERSON
पण्डितवग्गो

There is one way for acquiring things—the way of the childish; there is another way, leading to unbinding—the way of the skilled. How does a person begin to develop the skills necessary for awakening? In the same basic manner that a carpenter or musician develops the skills that those tasks require: by "regard[ing] the person who sees your faults as a revealer of treasures." By, furthermore, keeping company with that person—a master of the trade—and permitting him or her to "exhort, instruct, and restrain you from poor behavior."

While the actual skills differ, of course, from trade to trade and profession to profession, the fundamental process of developing skill does not. Whether you want to become a burglar or a *buddha*, you must, according to this chapter, fulfill the following steps: First, subject yourself to the training of an accomplished master of the trade. Second, avoid those who would discourage you in your quest, and seek out those who would encourage you. Finally, fully *internalize* the skills necessary for your trade, until they are "as a rock of single solid mass."

At this point, each trade will require quite particular skills. It is, in fact, the peculiar skills of each trade that define that trade and distinguish it from all others. This chapter—indeed the whole *Dhammapada*—makes clear that in the trade of awakening, skills such as restraint, mindfulness, forsaking of material acquisitions, renunciation of ambitious worldly goals, and balanced mental health are necessary. Similarly, each trade culminates in a distinct result. The culmination of the skills prescribed in the *Dhammapada* is the singular goal of Buddhism: serenity, "as a deep pond, clear, calm" . . . unbinding.

NOTES

76. *skilled person.* This term, the same one as in the chapter title, *paṇḍita,* is routinely translated as "wise" and "learned." But, as with other terms I have mentioned, Buddhists often used such everyday terms with specific, technical nuances. What quality *specifically* makes a person "wise"? Every tradition, every school of thought, will answer this question differently, depending on its view and aim. For Buddhists, the answer is skill. A person is wise or learned who is pursuing or has acquired the skills delineated in this chapter and throughout the *Dhammapada.*

77. *the good . . . the bad.* These translate *sata* and *asata* respectively. While I generally try to avoid such vague and moralistic sounding terms, in this case avoidance is not possible. The primary meaning of the verbal root *sat* is "to be." This easily gives way to "real" and "actual," and less obviously perhaps, "to be as anyone/thing *ought* to be"; namely, "good, honest, wise." (See note 190 on *sacca/satya* as "truth.")

78. *encouraging friends.* This is a translation of *kalyāṇamitta.* Having a friend to encourage you in the development of the skills necessary for awakening is considered of paramount importance in Buddhism. That friend must himself or herself possess certain traits, such as kindness, virtue, generosity, the ability to offer good advice—all of which are meanings of the term *kalyāṇa* itself.

79. *the way revealed by the noble ones.* "Noble ones" (*ariya*) are those who have embarked on the path to awakening, from "stream-enterers" to the "accomplished" (*arahant*). (See note 45.) Given the circular cosmology of India, it is perhaps not surprising that the Buddha understood his teachings to be but the most current expression of the "noble path" (*ariyamagga*). Notice the plural forms in the following verses.

> The Buddhas of the past,
> the future Buddhas,
> and he who is the Buddha now,
> removing the sorrow of many—

> all have dwelt, will dwell, and dwell,
> deeply revering the true Dhamma:
> for the Buddhas this is the natural law.
> (*Saṃyuttanikāya* 1.6, verses 562–563)

Since, in the Buddha's day, *ariya* would have been a clear allusion to the dominant Vedic culture, the original *arya* who migrated both westward and eastward (compare Eire, Ireland, and Iran with *arya*), this word usage may also be seen as another instance of the Buddha's appropriation and redefinition of important sociocultural markers.

85–86. *the other shore.* This is an often used metaphor for *nibbāna/nirvāṇa.* These two verses lay out two possibilities. The first is to remain one of the deluded people who, lacking insight into the four noble truths, constitute the bulk of humanity. The second is to become an awakened person, a *buddha,* one who by definition has "gone to the other shore of suffering" (*Saṃyuttanikāya* 1.8, verse 749; and see note 23).

86. *realm of death.* In a conversation with the Buddha, Māra succinctly reveals the cause of this bondage:

> That of which they say, "it is mine,"
> and those who speak in terms of "mine"—
> if your mind exists among these,
> you will not escape me, ascetic.
>
> (*Saṃyuttanikāya* 1.4, verse 500)

87–88. *from home to no home.* These two verses make plain the ascetic impulse of the earliest Buddhism. What starker image of the *pabbajjā,* the mendicant practitioner, could there be than that of one wandering in homelessness? (See note 74.)

89. *factors of full awakening.* One of the most important sections of the Pāli canon, in terms of its role as a receptacle of the Buddha's teachings, is the *Mahāvagga* ("The Great Section/Book"), part five of the *Saṃyuttanikāya.* What makes this section so significant is that it contains the teachings which later came to be known as the thirty-seven "qualities that are wings, or aids, to awakening" (*bodhipakkhiyadhamma*). (Readers who wish to explore further the seven sets of teachings the Buddha repeatedly maintained his disciples must train in [for example at *Majjhimanikāya* 103.2–4], see, in addition to the *Mahāvagga* itself, an illuminating book by Thanissaro Bhikkhu, *The Wings to Awakening* [Barre, Mass.: Dhamma Dana Publications, 1996].) Within these thirty-seven qualities are seven factors known as the *bojjhaṅga,* "the factors for awakening" (Sanskrit *bodhi* > Pāli *bojjha* + *aṅga*), that is, seven personal and practical qualities that *lead* the practitioner to awakening. The Buddha mentions the seven qualities in the following passage.

> [Someone approached the Buddha] and said to him, "venerable sir, it is said, 'factors of awakening, factors of awakening.' In what sense are they called factors of awakening?"

[The Buddha answered:] "They lead to awakening, therefore they are called factors of awakening. Here, one develops the awakening factor of mindfulness . . . of discrimination of states . . . of energy . . . of rapture . . . of tranquility . . . of concentration . . . of equanimity. (*Bojjhaṅgasaṃyutta*, "Connected Discourses on the Factors of Enlightenment," *Saṃyuttanikāya* 5.46.5)

89. *impulses*. This translates a fundamental Buddhist category, that of the *āsavas/āśravas*. This term has vexed many a translator of Buddhist literature, as can be gathered from its numerous renderings. Examples include "impurity," "defilement," "taints," "cankers," "effluents," "intoxicants," "influxes," "streams," "corruptions," "currents," and "flows." There are unfortunate examples as well: "evil influence," "Evil Cankers," "depravity," and "sin." Deriving from the verbal formation (prefix) *ā* + (root) *su,* the term means "to flow out." It is used to denote, for example, the flow of a river, the secretion of tree sap, the intoxicating extract of certain plants and flowers, and the ooze discharged from a sore.

Now, transfer these images from the natural or bodily realms to the psychological-existential sphere of life, and the Buddhist sense becomes clearer. The *āsavas* are the three, sometimes four, forces that propel a person through *saṃsāra*. Because they are considered to be so inextricably bound up with, so deeply rooted in, human existence, I have translated the term referring to them as "impulses." This word choice is meant to capture the sense of their being urges that occur prior to cognitive functions and are seemingly autonomous. I have also tried to retain the metaphorical flavor of the Pāli verb as involving drive and compulsion. The *āsavas* are the impulse toward sense desire (*kāmāsava*), the impulse toward becoming (*bhavāsava*), and the impulse toward ignorance (*avijjāsava*) (see *Dīghanikāya* 2.97). In some passages, a fourth is mentioned, the impulse toward views (*diṭṭhāsava*). The basic nature of these impulses is, in the Buddha's words, to "defile, bring renewal of being, give trouble, ripen in suffering, and lead to future birth, aging, and death" (*Majjhimanikāya* 36.47; see also *Sabbāsava*, "All the Taints," *Majjhimanikāya* 2).

CHAPTER SEVEN

THE ACCOMPLISHED PERSON

अरहन्तवग्गो

It is fitting that the last verse of the previous chapter, on skillfulness, gives a description of the culmination of skill: "such bright ones, impulses destroyed,/are, in this very world, unbound." This is a precise definition of the person who has mastered the skills of the Buddhist way. A person who has quieted the most deep-seated urges of existence—the impulses toward sense desire, becoming, and ignorance—which had been driving him or her from below the threshold of conscious awareness, is commonly said to have "lived the holy life, done what had to be done." Such a person is thereby "accomplished" (*arahant*). The *arahant*, the ideal practitioner type in early Buddhism and present-day Theravāda, is the subject of this chapter.

As if to suggest the difficulty of comprehending the qualities of an *arahant*, or perhaps in order to *create* such a difficulty as a way of fending off complacency, the text resorts to similes and metaphors. Like a crane never settling on the moor where, in passing, it seeks some nourishment, a person who has accomplished the Buddhist way *lets go* interminably. Such a person is like a bird gliding through space. He moves through life feeling, felt, and real, but the weight of "the burden" lifted, his haughty pretense of "I, me, and mine" stilled, he leaves no trace of himself. The accomplished person's senses have become as a tamed horse's. Though having the power to run wild and uncontrolled, they are, through their very restraint, serene. A common theme throughout these verses is the peace, calm, serenity, and delight of accomplishing the Buddhist way.

NOTES

90. *the knots removed.* The Buddha mentions four tendencies that knot up (*gantha*) a person, hindering development of the eightfold path. These four must be fully understood, destroyed, and abandoned.

> [Practitioners], there are these four knots. What four? The bodily knot of covetousness, the bodily knot of ill will, the bodily knot of distorted grasp of rules and vows, the bodily knot of adherence to dogmatic assertion of truth. (*Saṃyuttanikāya* 5.45.174)

91. *The mindful.* Practitioners who engage in the central Buddhist practice of *satipaṭṭhāna* (establishment of mindfulness). Such a practitioner persistently "dwells contemplating the body in the body, ardent, clearly comprehending, mindful, having removed covetousness and displeasure in regard to the world ... dwells contemplating feelings in feelings ... mind in mind ... phenomena in phenomena." (See note 21, "*the deathless.*")

92. *the nature of food.* Food seems harmless enough. Like breath, it is essential for survival. But, perhaps because of its importance, it may also serve as the focal point of mental and physical disease (bulimia, obesity), group dissension (in scarcity), social chaos and war (in famine). It is not difficult to imagine the importance of regulating the acquisition, distribution, and consumption of food in a community of beggars (the basic meaning of *bhikkhu*, the word for a Buddhist mendicant or, later, monk). (Readers interested in exploring these rules in more detail should refer to the *Vinaya* translations by I. B. Horner, *The Book of Discipline*, 6 vols. [London: Sacred Books of the East, 1938–1966].)

The statement here, on "the nature of food," refers to the nutriments, explained in note 93. But it might be helpful to relate here, for the benefit of a supersized America, the Buddha's recommended diet:

> Consume your food wisely, with care. [Eat] neither in order to pass the time, nor for enjoyment, nor to acquire beauty or charm. But [eat] merely for the purpose of maintaining and prolonging this body, in order to prevent illness, and as a means of supporting the holy life. (*Aṅguttaranikāya* 3.16)

93. *nutriments.* Existence is founded on and conditioned by nutriment or sustaining nutrition (*āhāra*). In the catechism-like *Saṅgīti Sutta*, "The Chanting

Together," which contains a comprehensive inventory of the teachings, the Buddha asks at the outset: "There was one thing that was perfectly proclaimed by the [Buddha], who knows and sees. . . . What is this one thing?" [Answer:] "All beings are maintained by nutriment" (*Dīghanikāya* 33.1.8 [1]). Specifically, the nutriments are edible food, contact, mental volition (will), and consciousness. Food sustains the body, the physical mode of being, while the other three sustain the psychological modes of being. (See *Saṃyuttanikāya* 2.12.63 for the proper attitude toward these, and *Majjhimanikāya* 38.15 for how they fit into the scheme of "dependent arising.")

97. *the unconditioned.* A synonym for *nibbāna/nirvāṇa.* It is unconditioned because it is not an object, which by definition possesses composite parts and is thus dependent on external, contributing causal factors. In a succinct definition of the unconditioned, the Buddha says: "And what is the unconditioned? The destruction of lust [passion], the destruction of hatred [aversion], the destruction of delusion. This is called the unconditioned" (*Saṃyuttanikāya* 4.43.2). For a full treatment of the unconditioned and the path to the unconditioned, see *Asaṅkhatasaṃyutta,* "Connected Discourses on the Unconditioned," *Saṃyuttanikāya* 4.43.

CHAPTER EIGHT

THOUSANDS

सहस्सवग्गो

Lacking in any technical vocabulary, and containing a single, straightforward message, this chapter provides a place of reflection between the more demanding verses that precede and follow. One of the purposes of reflection is to create clarity regarding the meaning of what one has read. Reflection also fosters selective attention, or focus. Not everything in a text is of equal value. Which of the ninety-nine verses and several thousand words that you have read so far must really be taken to heart? Which serve a secondary or supportive function? Which play a largely aesthetic role, creating a particular mood (*bhava*) or flavor (*rasa*) as background to the surrounding verses? Which are intended as rhetorical and structuring devices, effectively constituting the text's framework, the scaffolding for the teaching?

These matters are not easy to determine. And it is precisely this difficulty in sorting through the uneven offerings of not only the text itself but the world as a whole that this chapter addresses. The approach here is to encourage the reader to employ the method of reducing quantity and distilling quality. The purpose throughout is to achieve the effectiveness in practice that Buddhists refer to as "cultivation," rather than the mere appearance of development.

CHAPTER NINE

DETRIMENT

पापवग्गो

This chapter emphasizes the reality of detrimental actions and their effects. It implores the reader to scrutinize the movements of his or her thoughts, words, and body for any trace of destructive or damaging elements. For, like the slow accumulation of drops of water falling into a pot, our small, seemingly insignificant, everyday "misdeeds" gather force. But the observable reality of accumulated effect is not presented here as a deterministic fait accompli. In these verses, we meet again two important observations made by the Buddha that became crucial components of his teaching: (1) human beings' acute proneness to habit formation; and (2) the possibility of abandoning harmful forms of behavior and, conversely, of strengthening and developing beneficial ones. Finally, in case the scope and importance of the matter are lost on the reader, the chapter ends by evoking Buddhist images of space and time and asserting that there is no place to hide from the inevitable blossoming of one's actions.

The word in the title of this chapter that I am translating as "detriment" is *pāpa*. In Sanskrit drama, the *pāpaka* is the bad guy, the villain. Thus, in translations of Buddhist works, *pāpa* is normally rendered as "bad," "wrong," "evil," "wrongdoing," and even "sin" or "sinful." But, as might be expected, Buddhists have a more exact notion of what constitutes "bad" than such vague terms permit. As we saw in verses 66 and 67, an action is bad or wrong if it (1) produces a result stemming from one's actions—that is, from an actual situation or outcome—that is harmful, damaging, or destructive in any way ("bear[s] bitter fruit"); and (2) engenders a sense of remorse or shame after it has been committed ("one regrets"). "Bad" and "wrong" are, thus, matters not of strict, legalistic formulations or judgments from above but, rather, of subjective responses and *lived* consequences right where we are.

NOTES

Introduction to Chapter Nine. *possibility of abandoning.* See Thanissaro Bhikkhu, *The Wings to Awakening* (Barre, Mass.: Dhamma Dana Publications, 1996), pp. 21ff.

116. *detriment.* Pāli *pāpa*, and its several cognates, is translated in this chapter and elsewhere in the text in various ways, depending on the nuance of meaning and specificity called for by context: "detriment," "detrimental," "detrimental action," "misdeed," "harm," "harmful," "injury," "damage," "destructively," "bad," "troubling," "loss," "negativity," "misfortune."

116. *creates value.* This term, *puñña*, is usually translated as "merit" or "goodness." As verse 122 suggests, *puñña* is understood as a process that accumulates in force and is stored, like drops of water, in a pot. This image fits easily into the Buddha's understanding of the human psychological proclivity toward habit formation and the possibility of developing skills. Goodness generates goodness, creating a stream of goodness, which like a river nourishes everything around it. It can also be dipped into and spread around. The Buddha, in fact, often used metaphors of water to talk about his notion of accumulating goodness, as well as the unfathomable riches of such value creation.

> Just as the many rivers used by the hosts of people,
> flowing downstream, finally reach the ocean,
> the great mass of water, the boundless sea,
> the fearsome receptacle of heaps of gems;
> so, the streams of merit reach the wise man—
> giver of food, drink, and clothes,
> provider of beds, seats, and covers—
> as the rivers carry their waters to the sea.
>
> (*Saṃyuttanikāya* 5.55.41)

These verses refer to the merit, or value, of generosity, which is normally recommended for the laity in particular. Three additional "streams" are mentioned: confirmed confidence in the Buddha, the Dhamma, and the Saṅgha (*Saṃyuttanikāya* 5.55.42).

126. *the lower world . . . a higher world.* These are usually translated as "hell" and "heaven," respectively. Those renditions may suit a static Christian cosmology but certainly not the dynamic Buddhist one. Again, "hell" and "heaven" are not outright incorrect, but they do raise unnecessary problems. (See note 30, "*radiant ones,*" and the introduction to Chapter 22.)

CHAPTER TEN

VIOLENCE

दण्डवग्गो

This chapter presents three basic arguments, and intimates one extraordinary one. These arguments are against acting violently, or stated in positive terms, *for* putting down the burden of anger and aggression. The first argument is in the mode of that age-old ethical-religious dictum "Do unto others." Since you yourself have experienced, to some degree or another, the fear that violent behavior arouses, then, mindful of the feelings of others, refrain from it. When you do so, you are not only extending kindness to others but also protecting yourself from the consequences of angry responses. For, as the text bluntly states, "Those to whom you speak/might respond to you./Angry talk really is painful."

As this statement already suggests, another tack taken here is to appeal to our yearning for happiness, well-being, and ease. It is perhaps an observable fact that a person who goes through life speaking and acting and, according to the Buddha, even thinking, in aggressive ways does not typically enjoy a great deal of ease. The third argument presented in this chapter thus details somewhat this lack of peace by listing some of the consequences—observable and otherwise—of violent and aggressive tendencies, such as illness, mental problems, and desertion by family members.

Finally, verse 134 asks a provocative question that might be understood as the ultimate argument for refraining from aggression: is it possible that *nibbāna/nirvāṇa* is realized precisely in the nonresounding of aggressive impulses from within or without?

NOTES

136. *unthinking one.* This term (*dummedho*) appears numerous times in the *Dhammapada.* In translations of Buddhist works it is often rendered as "dullard," "stupid man," "ignorant," "idiot," "fool," "unintelligent," "dimwitted." Aside from amounting to some unkind name-calling, such terms miss the point. What is important is not brain capacity or intellectual ability but whether or not a person possesses a mature self-awareness.

141–142. *Neither naked wandering... a practitioner.* The Buddha disapproved not of austerity and asceticism as such but only of the extreme or exclusive reliance on them. An ascetic asks the Buddha whether it is true, as he had heard, that the Buddha "disapproves of all austerities, and censures and blames all those who lead a harsh life of self-mortification." The Buddha answers that he claims no such thing. One person practices austerities and sinks in fortune; another practices identical austerities and rises in fortune. The determining factor is not the intensity of the austerity but whether the practitioner has developed "non-enmity, non-ill-will and a heart full of loving-kindness" (*Dīghanikāya* 8; see also *Majjhimanikāya* 7.19–21 and *Majjhimanikāya* 40).

On my translation of Brahmin (*brāhmaṇa*), wanderer (*samaṇa*), and monk (*bhikkhu*) as "superior person," and "seeker," and "practitioner" respectively, see note 31, "*practitioner,*" and the introduction to Chapter Twenty-six.

142. *the lofty life.* This is a shorthand term (*brahmacariya*) for pursuing the entire Buddhist course of training.

144. *meditative concentration.* This translates the important Buddhist technical term *samādhi,* which is often rendered simply as "meditation." However, the attainment of *samādhi* is incomplete in itself. Its function is to create the mental stability that gives rise to "wisdom" (*paññā*), or direct insight (*vipassanā*) into the nature of the mind. As the Pāli term (affixes) *sam + ā +* (verbal root) *dhi* indicates, this stability involves a "thorough gathering together" of the diffused mind. A leading female follower of the Buddha, named Dhammadinnā, explained this point succinctly to one inquirer: "unification of mind is concentration [*samādhi*]" (*Majjhimanikāya* 44.12).

CHAPTER ELEVEN

OLD AGE

जरावग्गो

The tendency toward violence and aggression identified in the last chapter is detrimental to a person's well-being in obvious ways. Starkness is in the very nature of violence. But, as damaging as it is, physical, verbal, and mental aggression is at least forcefully and blaringly present for the practitioner to take note of. By contrast, aging and physical decay, the subjects of this chapter, are slow and barely discernible. Because of this fact, they may be even more menacing, for being so subtle, they can be denied. The body wears out; like gourds growing since late summer, it is cast off when the season turns cold and gray. The images in this chapter are simultaneously of strength, glory, and withering away. The body is a fortress, within which are concealed death and decay. Once, perhaps, as stunning and attractive to other people as the colorful chariot of the king, one's body eventually fades—like the colorful chariot of the king. These verses express in a stark fashion the importance that Buddhists place on countering the demands of the body, and checking our natural inclination to answer those demands. In this vein, the verses here can be read as an antidote to a major hindrance to awakening: being preoccupied with our bodies, as fleeting and frail as they are, at the expense of acquiring the treasure of insight, and freedom from the claims of death and decay.

NOTES

146. *when all is perpetually ablaze.* In a well-known text commonly referred to as the "Fire Sutta," the Buddha states repeatedly, "All is burning." In identifying the source and extent of the burning, he then names what constitutes the "proper range" of human existence—the extent and limit of experience. (See note 1–2, "*preceded by mind are phenomena.*")

> And what, is the all that is burning? The eye is burning, forms are burning, eye-consciousness is burning, eye-contact is burning, and whatever feeling arises with eye-contact as condition—whether pleasant or painful or neither-pleasant-or-painful. Burning with what? Burning with the fire of lust [passion], with the fire of hatred [aversion], with the fire of delusion; burning with birth, aging, and death; with sorrow, lamentation, pain, displeasure, and despair. The ear is burning, sounds are burning . . . the nose is burning, scents are burning . . . the tongue is burning, tastes are burning . . . the body is burning, tangible objects are burning . . . the mind is burning, thoughts are burning. . . . (*Saṃyuttanikāya* 4.35.28)

This passage comprises an abbreviated expression of the comprehensive Buddhist classification of lived experience, the "eighteen elements" (*dhātu*):

1. The six internal bases (*āyatana*) of consciousness, by means of which the "world" is "encountered": eyes, ears, nose, tongue, body, mind. Since the *khandhas* "world" (read as a verb), there is no preestablished, *khandha*-independent world to be uniformly encountered by beings. (See note 62.)
2. The six external bases of consciousness—that which is "encountered": form, sound, scent, taste, tangibility, thought.
3. The six consciousnesses that arise in this encounter: visual-consciousness, sound-consciousness, scent-consciousness, taste-consciousness, tactile-consciousness, and mental-consciousness. (See *Dhātusaṃyutta,* "Connected Discourses on Elements," *Saṃyuttanikāya* 2.14.)

This passage goes further by alluding to the Buddhist theory of causation known as "dependent arising" (*paṭiccasamuppāda*), which serves as an account of continued existence from moment to moment *and* from life to life ("birth, aging, and death"; see *Nidānasaṃyutta,* "Connected Discourses on Causation," *Saṃyuttanikāya* 2.12). It furthermore mentions the three "poisons" at the heart of this "chain of becoming": "passion, aversion, and delusion," as well the resulting condition, "sorrow, lamentation," et cetera.

153–154. *I have coursed through the whirl . . . the end of cravings.* There is a persistent legend, arising, probably, from the later commentarial tradition, that these two verses were the first words spoken by the Buddha immediately after his full awakening. (Readers interested in the commentary to the *Dhammapada* should refer to Eugene Burlingame, *Buddhist Legends: Translated from the Original Pāli Text of the Dhammapada Commentary* [Cambridge, Mass.: Harvard University Press, 1921], vols. 28–30. This work was reprinted for the Pali Text Society by Luzac and Co., London, 1960, parts 1–3.)

154. *free from the conditioned.* An epithet of *nibbāna / nirvāṇa.*

—ᘰᘰ—

CHAPTER TWELVE

ONESELF

अत्तवग्गो

Following a chapter that has just cautioned against being overly concerned with the body and its endless needs and demands, the present chapter teaches what may seem, at first glance, to contradict that very point: the vital importance of oneself for oneself. In the last chapter, the practitioner was warned against holding himself or herself too dear. The futility and waste of this self-absorption are presented in harsh terms. In the end, such a person will lie like a dry, aged heron in a lake with no water—the potential treasure of youth unrealized, the lofty life unlived. Here, holding oneself dear is presented as the very *beginning* of the "lofty life."

The difference, of course, is that in the former case concern for oneself is harmful to the cultivation of skills that lead to awakening because the focus is the fleeting instrument of the worldly, unthinking life. In the latter case, the focus shifts to the person who has the skill to realize that fact. So, in this sense, this chapter assumes that the reader has learned the lesson of the previous chapter and is now ready to take charge of himself or herself, to "attain the master" by *becoming* the master of oneself.

The verses here echo one of the final instructions of the Buddha to his disciples: "Live as islands (or lamps) unto yourselves, being your own refuge, with no one else as your refuge!" (*Dīghanikāya* 16.2.26). As commonsensical as it seems, for a practitioner of a teaching as psychologically methodical and phenomenologically oriented as Buddhism, failure or success hinges on one's ability to be one's own refuge, or, as verse 157 expresses it, to "take care of himself." This verse is a reminder that Buddhism, as it stands in early texts such as the *Dhammapada,* is not in the least oriented toward supernatural agency, divine grace, or any other such help from above.

CHAPTER THIRTEEN

THE WORLD
लोकवग्गो

This chapter continues in the exhortatory tone discernible in the previous two chapters. Assuming, however, an even sharper insight into the
problems presented in those verses, this chapter invites the reader to
enter more deeply into the way revealed in the *Dhammapada*. In a phrase
used by the Buddha to initiate practitioners into the order, the reader is
urged to "come, look." In this utterly simple exhortation, the Buddha is
challenging the hearer or reader to observe what is the case with the
world as it appears before his or her very awareness moment by moment.
The notion of a redemptive baptism or saving conversion is completely
foreign to the understanding expressed in this utterance.

Since the operative metaphor of the goal is *freedom from* rather than
redemption by, the *only* means of embarking on the way is to "come," fully
and wholly, onto the way; and the *only* way to cultivate the skills and insight necessary for awakening is to "look." What a person sees when he or
she looks is the world as mirage, and the ever-occurring appearances of
our lives as bubbles. But this is too easy to "see" intellectually; as an idea,
the dreamlike quality of the world is not difficult to grasp. To see it in the
sense of having "insight" into it, as the Buddha constantly implores, is
quite a different matter.

Unlike a mere conceptual understanding, insight into impermanence
cuts right through our deep emotional yearning for a stable, abiding
world. For this reason, the verses here distinguish between practicing the

teaching and practicing the teaching well. A powerful image is provided to depict the person who fulfills the latter. That person becomes one who has "enter[ed] the stream." That practitioner's efforts toward skillful cultivation have become forceful currents carrying him or her to freedom. Such a person illuminates the world, as does the moon when it has been freed from an obstructing cloud. And in case the sheer power of such a person's illumination has not been understood, the final verse makes it clear: the fruits of entering the stream are greater than dominion over the entire cosmos.

NOTES

170. *bubble . . . mirage.* See note 46.

171. *Come, look.* This may also be rendered "come and see." The usual form is the second-person singular imperative (Pāli: *ehi passa*); the form here is second-person plural imperative (*etha passatha*). The adjectival form (*ehipassika*) is commonly used as a description of the teaching as "inviting inspection." (See, for example, *Dīghanikāya* 24.1.6.) The careful reader has probably noticed the abundance of verbs of seeing in the *Dhammapada*. This usage of such verbs applies equally to other Buddhist literature extending throughout the history of the tradition.

176. *this single matter.* This phrase, *ekaṃ dhammaṃ*, can also be construed to refer broadly to the teaching as a whole: "this unique (*ekaṃ*) way or teaching (*dhammaṃ*)."

176. *false speech.* The Buddha had a great deal to say about the manner in which we speak to one another. His epithet, Sākyamuni/Śākyamuni (literally, "*silent* sage of the Sākya/Śākya clan"), must have been somewhat ironic or, more likely, in the vein of the numerous creative appropriations of pan-Indic terms in which the Buddha and his followers engaged. A fleeting glance at the discourses of the Buddha indicates just how important speaking was to him. His days were filled with teaching, conversing, debating, refuting, admonishing, and encouraging.

"Right speech" (*sammāvācā*) is a fundamental feature of the ethical component of the teaching. (See note 38.) It is glossed in the description of the eightfold path as "abstaining from false speech, abstaining from malicious speech, abstaining from harsh speech, abstaining from useless speech." Useless speech is sometimes further glossed as idle talk, trivial chatter, gossip, et cetera. Undertaking the training rule to abstain from false speech is also the fourth of the five basic precepts taken by lay Buddhists.

178. *entering the stream.* (See also note 45.) The Buddha offers the following succinct definition of "stream-entry." After briefly mentioning the "five aggregates of clinging" (form, feeling, perception, mental fabrication, and consciousness), he gives the criteria for achieving this stage of the path and mentions the certainty that ensues from its attainment, as well as its end:

> When a noble disciple understands as they really are the origin and the passing away, the gratification, the danger, and the escape in the case of these five aggregates subject to clinging, then that one is called a noble disciple who is a stream-enterer, no longer bound to a nether world [i.e., not subject to rebirth in a lower world], fixed in destiny, with awakening as his destination. (*Saṃyuttanikāya* 3.22.109)

This passage, in fact, refers to one of the three "fetters," the breaking of which constitutes stream-entry. In understanding the nature of the aggregates of clinging, the practitioner destroys the fetter of "self," i.e., the view that there is a substantial personality dwelling in the aggregates. The other two fetters that are destroyed are doubts about the Buddha's teaching and prescribed path, and overmuch confidence in the power of rules, vows, and rituals to "cause" liberation (see *Aṅguttaranikāya* 3.85). The four factors of stream-entry are "association with good people, hearing the true teaching, thorough attention, and practice of the teaching in its entirety" (*Dīghanikāya* 33.1.11 [13]).

CHAPTER FOURTEEN

THE AWAKENED

बुद्धवग्गो

The word in the chapter title that translates as "the awakened" is *buddha*. This could obviously be rendered simply as "the Buddha," as it in fact normally is. There are references in these verses to both the historical Buddha (taking refuge in *the* Buddha), and transhistorical *buddhas* ("happy is the appearance of awakened ones"). But, with the exception of occasional millennial trends in certain Buddhist communities, it is not the case that a full-blown Buddha *comes to* or *appears in* the world, in the sense of an "advent." Rather, people who "practice the teaching well," as earlier verses have indicated, and achieve the status of "stream-enterers" and so forth through careful cultivation of the teaching, *are* "the awakened."

Several of the verses in this chapter define just what it means to be awakened. It may be surprising to some readers that awakening is presented as a thoroughly attainable human goal. The person is awakened, for example, who is free from "ensnaring, entangling craving." The mindful person, the text says, *is* awakened; abiding in the refuge of the teaching *is* release from pain. Although there is admittedly a good deal involved in establishing such mindfulness, or in untangling oneself from the incessant pangs of desire, awakening is not presented here as a superhuman, much less supernatural, attainment. It is presented rather as a matter of acquiring the necessary skills: those which distinguish the common, deluded person from the rare, awakened one.

Now, however that may be, there are passages in this chapter, as in

Buddhist literature generally, that attempt to communicate something of the strangeness or "otherness"—for lack of better words—of awakening. In a beautiful passage from another canonical work, for example, we read:

> Where water, earth, heat, and air find no support,
> there burn no bright stars nor shines the sun,
> the moon sheds not her radiant beams—
> but yet the home of darkness is not there.
>
> When in the deep and silent hours of thought
> the holy sage attains [awakening]
> then he is well released from joy and pain.
> From form and from the formless he is freed.
>
> (*Udāna* 1.10)

Similarly, our text evokes the "placelessness" of awakening when it speaks of the "limitless sphere" that has been realized, rendering the awakened person "trackless." These should be understood as images not of other-worldliness but of the vast and wondrous potentiality of life in *this* world.

NOTES

Introduction to Chapter Fourteen. *Udāna* 1.10. I quote a slightly altered translation by the renowned scholar and monk, Paravahera Vajirañāna Mahāthera, *Buddhist Meditation in Theory and Practice* (1962; Kuala Lumpur: Buddhist Missionary Society, 1975), p. 480. This is an exemplary work on Buddhist methods of meditation as delineated in the Pāli canon.

179. *awakened.* One of the most baffling and unfortunate turns that Buddhism has been forced to undergo in its movement to the West is the introduction of "light" metaphors to render derivatives of the Sanskrit verbal root *budh*. The Sanskrit and Pāli word *buddha*, a past passive participle of this root, simply means "awakened." The noun *bodhi*, the word from which we get the common English translation "enlightenment," means "awakening." All derivatives and usages of this term that denote something other than "waking up" invariably carry meanings of cognitive activity, such as discerning, understanding, becoming aware of, recognizing. Thus, if we must extend the senses of *buddha* and *bodhi*, it should be in this direction: the awakened person has undergone a cognitive, perhaps even epistemological, reorientation; that person's awakening has a cognitive, perhaps even epistemological, coloring. There is no hint of *light* in any of this.

Now, that is not to say that there is no use of light imagery in Buddhist literature to describe both the Buddha and his awakening. We have already seen some of this in the *Dhammapada*. But I suspect that such allusions are not the source of the oft-encountered designations "the Enlightened One" and "Enlightenment." Rather, I would expect to locate the beginnings of these terms in the early writings of Western admirers, scholarly and otherwise, who saw in the Buddha their ideal of the rational, nondogmatic sage of the eighteenth-century European Enlightenment. In any case, it would probably be too pedantic to ask readers to discontinue the use of these questionable and, when you think about it, misleading terms—but it would be good!

182. *Difficult is the attainment of a human birth.* This theme of the uniqueness of human birth persists throughout the history of Buddhism. In both Mahāyāna and Vajrayāna, for example, the practitioner is asked to reflect on the preciousness of human life as a means of stimulating resoluteness to practice.

183. *The refraining from all that is harmful.* In Theravādan countries, this verse is considered a summary of the Buddha's teachings.

189–190. *refuge.* In ancient India, taking refuge in the king or local ruler was an implicit acceptance of a reciprocal relationship. The ruler provided protection; the person taking refuge vowed loyalty. Buddhists use the metaphor of "going for refuge" as an expression of seriousness of intention on the side of the practitioner. The other side of the relationship, the awakened (*buddha*), the teachings (*dhamma*), and the community of practitioners (*sangha*), known collectively as "the three jewels" because of their extraordinary value, is then understood as having the capacity to provide shelter, security, and fortification. The difference between this metaphorical use of "refuge" and actual political or military refuge is of course that there is no notion here of an intervening external power. The three jewels provide refuge in that, through "practicing well," a person protects himself or herself from the pain of passion, aversion, delusion, grasping, and so on (as the following verses suggest).

In several instances, the Buddha equates "going for refuge" with becoming a lay disciple. Once a fellow Sakyan came to him and asked, "How, lord, is one a lay follower?" The Buddha replied, "If one has gone for refuge to the Buddha, Dhamma, and Sangha, then one is a lay follower" (*Anguttaranikāya* 8.25).

190. *the four noble truths.* These are not only the central teaching of the Buddha but also the template on which all subsequent Buddhist teachings are founded. In what is held by tradition to have been the Buddha's first public teaching, he proclaimed the four noble truths as follows. (On my translation of *dukkha*

as "pain," rather than the usual but overly severe term "suffering," see note 1–2, "*pain . . . ease*")

1. This is the noble truth of pain: birth is pain, aging is pain, illness is pain, death is pain; union with what is displeasing is pain; separation from what is pleasing is pain; not to get what one wants is pain; in brief, the five aggregates subject to clinging are pain.

2. This is the noble truth of the origin of pain: it is this craving which leads to renewed existence, accompanied by delight and lust, seeking delight here and there; that is, craving for sensual pleasures, craving for existence, craving for extermination.

3. This is the noble truth of the cessation of pain: it is the remainderless fading away and cessation of that same craving, the giving up and relinquishing of it, freedom from it, nonreliance on it.

4. This is the noble truth of the way leading to the cessation of pain: it is the noble eightfold path [see note 191]. (*Dhammacakkappavattana Sutta*, "The Discourse Setting in Motion the Wheel of the Doctrine," *Saṃyuttanikāya* 5.56.11)

These truths are "noble" (*ariya;* see note 236, "*noble ones*") because their realization constitutes attainment, and eventual completion, of the path. A person who sees them clearly is "a noble one," that is, one who is "devoid of covetousness, devoid of ill will, unconfused, clearly comprehending, ever mindful," et cetera (see *Aṅguttaranikāya* 3.65). These are "truths" (*sacca*) not because the Buddha has declared them so but because they are *observable.* The Sanskrit term *satya,* from which the Pāli *sacca* is derived, stems from the verbal root *sat.* The primary meanings of this verb are "to be," "to exist," "to be present." So, far from being proclaimed as "true" in a dogmatic or theoretical sense, each of the noble truths is posited by the Buddha to be *present* as a recognizable facet of human existence.

191. *the noble eightfold path.* The eight components of the path are subdivided into three main aspects of Buddhist training: morality, concentration, and wisdom. The path is defined at *Dīghanikāya* 22.21 as follows (see also the introduction to Chapter Twenty):

WISDOM

1. Right View: the knowledge of suffering, its origin, its cessation, and the way of practice leading to its cessation (the four noble truths)

2. Right Thought: the thought of (or aspiration for) renunciation, non-ill-will, harmlessness

MORALITY

3. Right Speech: refraining from lying, from slander, from harsh speech, and from frivolous speech
4. Right Action: refraining from taking life, from taking what was not given, and from sexual misconduct
5. Right Livelihood: refraining from any forms of livelihood that would compromise fulfillment of all other aspects of the eightfold path

CONCENTRATION

6. Right Effort: the practitioner (a) strives to *prevent* harmful mental states from arising; (b) strives to *overcome* those harmful, unwholesome mental states that have arisen; (c) strives to *produce* beneficial mental states that have not arisen; and (d) strives to *maintain* and *fully develop* beneficial, wholesome mental states that have arisen.
7. Right Mindfulness: "Here a [practitioner] dwells contemplating the body in the body, ardent, clearly comprehending, mindful, having removed covetousness and displeasure in regard to the world. He dwells contemplating feelings in feelings . . . mind in mind . . . phenomena in phenomena."
8. Right Concentration: attainment of the four states of meditative absorption (*jhāna*)
   a. Detached from sense-desires, detached from unwholesome mental states, the practitioner enters and remains in the first *jhāna*, which is with thinking and pondering, born of detachment, filled with delight and joy.
   b. With the subsiding of thinking and pondering, by gaining inner tranquillity and oneness of mind, the person enters the second *jhāna*, which is without thinking and pondering, born of concentration, filled with delight and joy.
   c. With the fading away of delight, remaining imperturbable, mindful, and clearly aware, the person experiences the joy of which the noble ones say, "Happy is the person who dwells with equanimity and mindfulness," and enters that third *jhāna*.
   d. Having given up pleasure and pain, and with the disappearance of former gladness and sadness, the person enters and remains in the fourth *jhāna*, which is beyond pleasure and pain, and purified by equanimity and mindfulness.

195. *obsessive activity and complexity.* This translates the Buddhist technical term *papañca*. This term is extremely important for understanding Buddhism; and it is extremely difficult to translate. To give some indication of each of these issues, I ask the reader to consider this translation/gloss by a contemporary Buddhist studies scholar. Bear in mind that this is an excellent translation,

particularly in terms of conceptual compactness and precision of meaning, and one that is hard to improve on: *papañca* is "the psycho-linguistic pro-liferation of cognitive-conative projections onto experience; or the linguistic 'excess' responsible for and resulting from mistaking interpretation for 'reality'" (Dan Lusthaus, *Buddhist Phenomenology* [London: Routledge-Curzon, 2002], p. 55). Illuminating—but impossible to fit into a pithy verse!

As this translation indicates, *papañca* has the basic meaning of the following notions: manifestation, development, manifoldness, diversity, diffuseness. All of this gives rise to another sense of the term: phenomena, appearance, the visible world, the expansion of the universe. Now, add these to a third sense of the word—deceit, fraud, trick, error, unreality—and the meaning may start to become apparent.

First, *papañca* is something that we *do* when we begin the very process of thinking and conceptualizing about the world, about things, situations, ideas, hopes, concerns, and so forth. In so doing, we *create* complication by projecting onto bare phenomena complex interpretations. Second, this interpretation is formed out of *our* proclivities—it does not arise out of the things, et cetera. Third, *papañca* is thus a mechanism of "worlding" (read as a present progressive verb). It is a process whereby a very particular world, *my* world, arises before *me*. This world is particular because it is dependent on my specific conceptual, linguistic, psychological, et cetera, structuring patterns. Fourth, all of this is, according to the Buddha, both personally and socially "besetting."

> Dependent on the eye and forms, eye-consciousness arises [through the eighteen *dhātus*; see note 146]. The meeting of the three is contact. With contact as condition there is feeling. What one feels, that one perceives. What one perceives, that one thinks about. What one thinks about, that one mentally proliferates [*papañca*]. With what one has mentally proliferated as the source, perceptions and notions [born of] mental proliferation beset a person with respect to past, future, and present forms cognizable through the eye [to mind-objects cognizable through the mind].
>
> (*Majjhimanikāya* 18.16)

> [The Buddha is asked:] "What gives rise to jealousy and avarice, what is their origin, how are they born, how do they arise? Owing to the presence of what do they arise; owing to the absence of what do they not arise?"
>
> [The Buddha responds:] "Jealousy and avarice take rise from like and dislike, this is their origin, this is how they are born, how they arise. When these are present, they arise. When these are absent, they do not arise."
>
> [Question:] "But what gives rise to like and dislike ... [as above]?"

[Answer:] "They arise from desire . . ."
[Question:] "But what gives rise to desire . . . ?"
[Answer:] "Desire arises from thinking. When the mind thinks about something, desire arises; when the mind thinks about nothing, desire does not arise."
[Question:] "But what gives rise to thinking . . . ?"
[Answer:] "Thinking arises from the tendency to proliferation [*papañca*]. When this tendency is present, thinking arises; when it is absent, thinking does not arise." (*Dīghanikāya* 21.2.2)

As the reader might surmise from these passages, an awakened person is defined in part by his or her ending of the process of *papañca* (see verse 254). An awakened person no longer tells stories about the world, no longer generates complexity, no longer engages in obsessive activity.

Interested readers should see Bhikkhu Ñāṇananda, *Concept and Reality in Early Buddhist Thought* (Kandy: Buddhist Publication Society, 1971).

—ా⌒ా—

CHAPTER FIFTEEN

BEING AT EASE

सुखवग्गो

Much of what Buddhism has to say appears so commonsensical as to be hardly worth mentioning. We read in a verse in this chapter, for instance, that defeating a person in some sense—being "right" or "better" are everyday examples—serves only to make that person ill at ease; thus, "victory begets hostility." Even a four-year-old child can see that. It is obvious, both practically and intellectually. Can it be that the great "wisdom of the East" preaches such platitudes? Maybe this is what one scholar of the *Dhammapada* had in mind when he denigrated the "insipid mediocrity" of many of its verses.

Yet, as commonsensical as these verses may *sound*, try to put them to practice. What happens? It should be clear to the reader by now that Buddhism is through and through concerned with *efficacy*. In place of the theory, belief, faith, and adherence to dogma that many other traditions assert as essential to participation in a religious life, here we find prescriptions for actual practices. Thus, I encourage the reader to consider the verses in this chapter in light of the Buddhist concern for transformative results; results, namely, that constitute the shift from a "deluded" to an "awakened" person. What would it mean, for instance, to live "relaxed amid the anxious"? What would the actual, *lived* effect be? The claim in this chapter is that the effect would be "ease," *sukha,* the opposite of *dukkha,* pain. As simple a concept as that may be, you cannot think your way to it. Try, rather, to live peacefully in the hostile world, or contentedly amid those who are being swept away in a "torrent of money" and possessions (verse 186). That is the ultimate wealth. That is the way *to be* at ease.

NOTES

Introduction to Chapter Fifteen. *"insipid mediocrity."* John Brough, *The Gāndhārī Dharmapada* (London: Oxford University Press, 1962), p. xvii. See Introduction under "Genre, Use, and Themes."

197. *ease.* My reasoning for this translation of *sukha* in place of the usual "happiness" is similar to that in note 66–67. Although the English word "happiness" does not carry moralistic undertones, it does miss the point somewhat. The verses here imply that for a person to experience "happiness," the conditions for "ease" must have been established. So, being at ease is primary, it precedes any "happy" feelings that one might experience.

201. *ill at ease.* This translates *dukkha.*

202. *the aggregates.* The *khandhas,* the instruments of grasping and clinging to the impermanent, nonsubstantial, and hence painful world of phenomena. The common word for this collection is "person." (See notes 60, *"round of birth and death,"* 62, 178.)

203. *Fabrications.* This is *saṅkhāra,* the same term for the fourth of the five *khandhas* (see previous note and in particular note 62). In this verse, it refers to "conditioned things," literally things that are "made together," that is, fashioned, constructed, produced from parts. This constructedness encompasses the entire phenomenal world, from subatomic particles to the universe (see also verses 277–279).

―ॐॐ―

CHAPTER SIXTEEN

PLEASING

पियवग्गो

According to Buddhism, one of the major sources of conflict, internal and external, personal and social, is the notion of "pleasing." When asked to explain the origin of "jealousy and avarice" in the world, the Buddha responded, "Jealousy and avarice have their origin in pleasing and not-pleasing," using the same word in the title of this chapter, *piya*, and its opposite, *appiya* (*Dīghanikāya* 21.2.2). The scope of these terms, to give the reader a better sense of their meaning, would allow them to be rendered as dear–not dear, pleasant-unpleasant, agreeable-disagreeable, like-dislike. The point in these verses is that trouble begins the moment we begin to like or dislike some object, person, or situation. Seeking what is pleasing, avoiding what is not pleasing, wanting, liking, being attached to, craving, holding on to, pushing away, not wanting, having aversion to, disliking, being disgusted by, loving, hating—what a dizzying, disconcerting, disappearing, disappointing whirl! Later (verse 402), we will be encouraged to "put down the burden and [be] free." Here we are shown, or really reminded of, the pitfalls of "pleasing."

NOTES

212. *springs from.* This observation that Z originates in Y is an important feature of the Buddhist view of causality. It is found most prominently in the teach-

ing on dependent arising (*paticcasamuppāda;* see *Nidānasaṃyutta,* "Connected Discourses on Causation," *Saṃyuttanikāya* 2.12). The basic idea is that *this,* Z, arises because *that,* Y, has arisen; Y has arisen in dependence on X, X in dependence on W, and so on. When *that* ceases to arise, *this* does not occur. (The example in the text in this: a liking arises, and this gives rise to an undercurrent of fear, however subtle or latent. If that liking does not arise, there is nothing to condition this fear.)

This process should not be understood as necessitating a strict, deterministic relationship between any two factors. In brief, because it involves causal factors from past *and* present, the number of actual possible outcomes of the interaction between X and Y is too vast to predict; hence, it is not deterministic. My "liking" has been causally conditioned over time, and it can be accounted for in numerous ways—culturally, psychologically, physiologically, and so on—all of which intersect with one another. These factors, furthermore, are undergoing constant change themselves. So, between the *this* and the *that* there are many potentially influencing factors. Nonetheless, as a guide to living, the logic of *paticcasamuppāda* is effective in its simplest formulation: if you want to stop smoking, just don't touch a cigarette.

Interested readers should consult Thanissaro Bhikkhu, *The Wings to Awakening* (Barre, Mass.: Dhamma Dana Publications, 1996), particularly pages 10–12.

218. *the nameless.* A term for *nibbāna/nirvāṇa.*
218. *"one who is streaming upward."* This is the third of the four stages of the path. The first three are referred to as the "three streams": stream-enterer, oncereturner, and non-returner, which is alluded to here (*uddhaṃsoto*). The final stage is *arahant* (see note 45). The Buddha gives this brief description of the non-returner (*anāgāmī*):

> The [practitioner] named so-and-so has died; the Blessed One has declared of him: "With the destruction of the five lower fetters he has reappeared spontaneously [in the Pure Abode—see note 30, *"radiant ones"*] and there will attain final *nibbāna* without ever returning from that world."
> (*Majjhimanikāya* 68.11)

The five coarse fetters alluded to in this passage are (1) the view or belief that there is a substantial personality dwelling in the aggregates; (2) doubts about the Buddha's teaching and prescribed path; (3) overmuch confidence in the power of rules, vows, and rituals to lead to liberation; (4) the impulse toward sensual desire; and (5) ill will toward others (*Dīghanikāya* 33.2.1 [7]).

_⌒◦⌒_

CHAPTER SEVENTEEN

ANGER

कोघवग्गो

In a graphic yet perfectly realistic description, the Buddha says that there is a type of person who "has a mind like an open sore." Why? "He is one who is irascible and irritable. If he is criticized even slightly he loses his temper and becomes angry and upset; he is stubborn and displays anger, hatred, and resentment. Just as, for instance, a festering sore, if struck by a stick or a shard, will discharge matter all the more, even so is the person who is irascible and irritable" (*Anguttaranikāya* 3.25). The verses in this chapter remind the reader of the necessity to guard against, restrain, conquer, and throw off the destructive emotion of anger. Buddhist discussions of anger almost invariable employ such violent language, as if anger were a monstrous beast to be slain. A radiant being asked the Buddha:

> Having slain what, does one sleep soundly?
> Having slain what, does one not sorrow?
> What is the one thing, O Gotama,
> whose killing you approve?
>
> Having slain anger, one sleeps soundly;
> having slain anger, one does not sorrow.
> The killing of anger, O radiant being,
> with its poisoned root and honeyed tip:
> this is the killing that the noble ones praise.
> For having slain that, one does not sorrow.
>
> (*Saṃyuttanikāya* 1.1.71 [223–224])

And, as if the necessity of slaying this beast is so obvious as to require no further convincing of the reader, this chapter begins with a clear and straightforward suggestion: just give up being angry.

NOTES

221. *body and mind.* This translates the technical term *nāmarūpa.* The English word "name" is a cognate of *nāma.* The most common meaning of *rūpa* is "form." Thus, *nāmarūpa* is often translated as "name and form." This is the term that the Buddha uses to designate what is commonly called the "person." Other renderings that adequately capture the meaning are "mentality-materiality," "psycho-physical organism," and "psychophysical personality." In their Buddhist technical usages, in short, *nāma* denotes the mental processes that are present in each moment of conscious experience, and *rūpa* refers to that which is derived from the four elemental physical properties of earth, water, fire, and air (see *Dīghanikāya* 33.1.11 [16]). Bhikkhu Bodhi's translation of these elements as "solidity, cohesion, heat, and distension" reveals something of their actual function in forming and maintaining matter (see Bhikkhu Bodhi, *The Middle Length Discourses of the Buddha: A Translation of the Majjhima Nikāya* [1995; Boston: Wisdom Publications, 2001], p. 1187, n. 129). A definition given by the Buddha is as follows:

> And what is *nāmarūpa?* Feeling, perception, volition, contact, and attention—these are called *nāma* [mentality, mind]. The four great elements and the material derived from the four great elements—these are called *rūpa* [materiality, form, body]. (*Majjhimanikāya* 9.54)

You will notice that the first three factors are the same as the mental *khandhas,* excluding consciousness. Consciousness and *nāmarūpa* have a reciprocal relationship. As it says further in the *sutta* passage just quoted, "With the arising of consciousness there is the arising of *nāmarūpa;* with the cessation of consciousness there is the cessation of *nāmarūpa.*" If, for instance, body and mind are present in a womb but consciousness is not, *nāmarūpa* (the baby) "will not come to birth." If consciousness is "cut off" in one's life, then *nāmarūpa* will not "grow, develop, and mature" (*Dīghanikāya* 15.21). The converse, however, is true as well. Body and mind, *nāmarūpa,* also condition consciousness: "When there is *nāmarūpa* consciousness comes to be" (*Saṃyuttanikāya* 2.12.65). That is, consciousness "finds its resting place in *nāmarūpa.*" (*Dīghanikāya* 15.22). Without body and mind, where could consciousness come to be? Additionally, there are contact and attention. "Contact" is when a bodily sense faculty "touches" its object (i.e., the eye meets the visible object; see note 13–14). "Attention" means "applying one's mind and attending to something" (*Dīghanikāya* 28.6). It thus refers simply to the quality of awareness that is present in any instance of conscious experience.

223. *Win over an angry person.* It is not clear to me that the Pāli necessarily has the ethical sense I have given it here. The verse could equally be translated as referring to a method of altering one's own harmful dispositions, as follows. Perhaps the ambiguity is intentional.

> Conquer anger with poise.
> Conquer meanness with kindness.
> Conquer greed with generosity,
> and false speech with honesty.

225. *that unshakable place.* A synonym for *nibbāna/nirvāṇa.*

227. *Atula.* This is a proper name. For the background story mentioning Atula, see Eugene Burlingame, *Buddhist Legends: Translated from the Original Pāli Text of the Dhammapada Commentary* (Cambridge, Mass.: Harvard University Press, 1921), vol. 30, pp. 113–115.

231–233. *bodily . . . verbal . . . mental misconduct.* Bodily misconduct is threefold: killing, taking what is not given, and engaging in socially and legally prohibited sexual activity. Verbal misconduct is fourfold: false speech, malicious speech (including divisive speech), harsh speech, and gossip. Mental misconduct is threefold: covetousness, ill will, and cruelty. In each case, the act is detrimental in that it "causes unwholesome states to increase and wholesome states to diminish in one who cultivates it." (See a detailed explanation of this three-fold conduct at *Majjhimanikāya* 114.)

CHAPTER EIGHTEEN

TOXINS

मलवग्गो

Purity is a concern exhibited by all religions. Religious initiation rites typically involve practices suggestive of cleansing, such as the sprinkling of water or full body immersion in water. Usually, even before the actual ceremony, the initiate must cleanse his or her body through adhering strictly to the dietary restrictions of the community. The water, too, is purified through various rituals, such as the uttering of special words over it (prayers, *mantras*), while making special gestures (the sign of the cross, *mudrās*). In many traditions, ablutions of some sort must be performed before daily ritual obligations can be fulfilled. The places where rituals are practiced, whether home altars or specially designated buildings, must be kept meticulously purified of both actual dirt and, more important, malevolent invisible forces. The same is true for ritual utensils, icons, clothing, officiants, and so on. An important dimension of religion then is the multilayered system of ritual practices employed to assure purity and cleanliness.

The Buddha often warned against replacing self-cultivation techniques, such as meditation and mindfulness, *exclusively* with ritualized practices, such as devotional worship and recitation of protective "spells." Although he did not prohibit such practices as long as they help engender constructive states of mind, he saw a danger in placing overmuch confidence in the power of rules, vows, and rituals to lead directly to liberation.

If we adopt a looser definition of "ritual," however, we can observe numerous cleansing rituals in the early Buddhist order. For example, the prohibition on eating after noon might be understood as a dietary rule related to concerns of bodily purity. The practice of shaving the head periodically may be seen as enhancing hygiene. In fact, the first act of the Buddha after he had left his home to pursue the life of a wandering seeker (*samaṇa*) was to cut off his hair. This act not only symbolizes renunciation of worldly values and ways but points to the new standard of bodily and mental purity required for the "lofty life" (*brahmacariya*). In ancient India long luxurious hair simultaneously indicated entanglement with the impure world *and* entangled one in that world.

With that knowledge as the background, it may be easier to appreciate this chapter on "toxins." In the Pāli title, the word is *mala*. This is normally translated as "impurity," "blemish," "stain," "dust," or "dirt." I have translated it in several ways here depending on the context. The underlying meaning throughout, as well as for those terms just mentioned, is "toxin." Other renderings in the verses in this chapter include "dross," "rust," and "taint."

The basic notion of a toxin as an impure element causing illness or imbalance is well summarized in verse 239:

> Gradually, little by little, moment by moment,
> the wise person should flush toxins from himself,
> as a metalsmith cleanses dross from silver.

This is an image of impurity as an adventitious condition. When the dross is cleaned off, what emerges is that which was there all along: silver. The impurity was not endemic to the silver but came afterward somehow. This simile also makes clear that care and patience must be taken to effect the purification. No mere ritual of silver purification can achieve *actual* cleansing of the silver object. Therefore, other, quite specific, skills are required for "flushing," namely, those skills that have recurred throughout the *Dhammapada*. So, inherent in the definition of "wise person" is the very recognition of the necessity to "flush toxins from himself," as well as the ability to do so. But what is meant by the phrase "from himself," and what is it that is called a "toxin" here? Elsewhere, the Buddha makes a significant statement in this regard concerning the nature of the mind as inherently pure yet the seat of "defilements" (or of what I am translating as "impulses"; see note 89, "*impulses*").

> This mind is luminous, but it is defiled by adventitious defilements. The uninstructed worldling does not understand this as it really is; therefore, for him there is no mental development. (*Aṅguttaranikāya* 1.6.1)

Toxicity, however, does not end "in" the mind. Remember the very first verse of the *Dhammapada?*

> If with mind polluted
> one speaks or acts,
> then pain follows,
> as a wheel follows
> the draft ox's foot.

Originating in the mind, toxins spread through every aspect of our lives. This chapter reveals that danger, encourages us to be on guard, and teaches us how to eliminate skillfully the toxins that poison those around us and slowly kill us just as we speak, think, and act.

NOTES

236. *noble ones.* The Buddha's appropriation of the term *ariya.* The Brahmins designated themselves "noble" in distinction to the "ignoble" indigenous peoples they had encountered on migrating to India a thousand years before the Buddha. As elsewhere, the Buddha completely undermines, in playful yet provocative ways, the original intent of the usage of the term. The "divine realm of the noble ones" refers, of course, not to the sacred lands of the Brahmins, or any sort of static heavenly world, but to attaining the status of non-returner or *arahant.* The "divine realm of the noble ones" may thus also refer to the understanding that non-returner status does entail the mental-cosmological consequence of "dwelling" in the five "pure abodes"/fourth plane of meditative absorption. (See notes 30, "*radiant ones,*" and 218, "*one who is streaming upward.*" For an expanded account of the "ten noble abodes," see *Aṅguttaranikāya* 10.20.)

238. *Fashion a lamp for yourself.* This is reminiscent of the final instructions of the Buddha to his disciples: "Live as lamps [or islands, *dīpa*] unto yourselves, being your own refuge, with no one else as your refuge!" (*Dīghanikāya* 16.2.26). See the introduction to Chapter Twelve.

254. *obsessive activity and complexity.* See note 195.

254. *Buddhas.* The actual Pāli word here is *tathāgata.* This is a somewhat enigmatic synonym for the Buddha or, as in this case, the plural, Buddhas. It means something like "those who have gone thus" (to awakening?).

CHAPTER NINETEEN

FIRMLY ON THE WAY

धम्मट्ठवग्गो

This chapter describes the person who has made good progress in eliminating the toxic ways of being that were addressed in the previous chapter. It begins by saying what such a person is *not*. To that end, some signposts are erected for the reader here—along the way—to indicate that he or she may not be so *firmly* on the way after all. While there is a slightly humorous tone to some of these verses, they may also deliver a bit of a sting. The reason is that we might see something of ourselves so clearly in them, something of the caricature Buddhist whose concern for external displays of personal identity has come at the expense of deeper internalization of Buddhist principles.

For example, the reader is reminded here that shaving his head and wearing the clothing of a seeker does not make him one; it just makes him look like one! Or just the fact that you have been around for a long time, your hair turning gray, does not mean that you are a venerable, wise person; it simply means that you are getting old! Just because you bum off of your friends and family does not mean that you are a *bhikkhu* (literally meaning "bum" or "beggar"; figuratively, "monk"). Furthermore, a tendency to talk effusively about Buddhist doctrines not only is *not* a sign of progress, but *is* a sign of regress; there is no idling on the Buddhist path. The converse is also true: silence does not make the sage, regardless of the common, clichéd image many of us have of such an "enlightened" one.

Being firmly on the way is quite a different matter from *appearing* to be so. The descriptions in the following verses depict the person who is firmly on the way as one of great emotional maturity: he or she is judicious, patient, composed, kind, and gentle. These are dispositions that can be neither imitated nor hurried. How then is firmness on the way achieved? The answer given here is simple: observe the teaching with your body. What follows from that plain imperative? What is seen, what is observed, when the teaching is *embodied*?

NOTES

259. *observes the teaching.* My translation of *passati*, "he sees," as "he observes" is intended to bring out the double sense of observation: seeing (directly realizing) and following (as is indicated in the next line).

260. *venerable.* The word here is *thera*. This is the first term in the name Theravāda, which means "doctrine of the elders" or, less concisely but more revealing of the actual sense of the term, "the exposition of the Buddha's doctrine based on the teachings of the firm seniors of the order."

265. *called a "seeker."* A complicated play on words is at work in this verse. In brief, because of the history of Pāli morphology, the word *samana* ("seeker") appears to be a derivative of the Sanskrit verbal root *śam*, "to still, calm, bring to peace." However, the meaning of *samana* is consonant with the Sanskrit *śramana*, which derives from the Sanskrit verbal root *śram*, "to wander." Enter into this the term found in our verse, *samitatta*, "the state of being stilled," which *is* derived from Sanskrit *śam*. Thus, the Pāli term *samana* is imbued with meanings arising out of this dual derivation of "wandering" and "stilling." It does not matter that this understanding is based on what philologists call a "false etymology." What is important for the reader to understand is the usage and meaning accorded the term by Buddhists, no matter how creative, or historically "inaccurate," that might be.

Another illuminating play on the word *samana* as "one who is in tune" has been pointed out by Thanissaro Bhikkhu in *The Wings to Awakening* (Barre, Mass.: Dhamma Dana Publications, 1996), pp. 26–27, 59.

266. *monk.* Early in the history of Buddhism the term *bhikkhu* came to signify a cloistered practitioner, hence the Greek derivative "*monk*." In the days of the Buddha himself, however, *bhikkhus* wandered from place to place, settling down temporarily only during the rainy season, when the roads became impassable. But even after they had established permanent settlements, "monasteries" (*vihāra*), they continued to beg alms for sustenance (see note 361).

268. *silence.* The verse plays on a word here, *muni,* that is common to the ancient Indian *samaṇa* traditions. The term is, in fact, the same as the second element in the Buddha's epithet, Śākyamuni (Pāli "Sakyamuni," though rarely used), the "sage of the Śakya" peoples. Really, it means "silent one." The idea is that those who possess *real* wisdom do not speak, since language invariably misrepresents "truth," while those who only pretend to wisdom are quick to proclaim it to others. The Buddha warns against this notion here. Wisdom consists in knowing when to speak and when to keep silent, when to elaborate and when to be brief.

270. *who harms living beings is not noble.* The *ariya,* or "noble ones" (see notes 22, 79, and 236, "*noble ones*"), prided themselves on their prowess as warriors. Thus, in common usage an *ariya* is precisely one who is *adept* at harming living beings.

CHAPTER TWENTY

THE PATH

मग्गवग्गो

At the heart of every religious tradition is a particular conception concerning the means by which the practitioner reaches the goal as conceived by that tradition. This is called "soteriology." Etymologically, this word is related to the terms "salvation" and "salve." As these meanings indicate, soteriology is that which is held to constitute the ultimate healing and health of a human being. A tradition's soteriology is related to two factors. The first is its notion concerning the most worthy, and most final, goal of human life, such as eternal heaven, liberation from the "small self," dissolution into the bliss-love that is the godhead, union with God, interminable rebirth as a compassionate human being, and so on. The second factor in determining soteriology is the view held by the tradition concerning the human condition, i.e., that which is fundamentally wrong, *the* existential problem confronting us: original sin, ignorance, fallenness, obscured bliss, and so on.

Each of these posited religious problems and ends entails specific responses. If the human illness is original sin and the goal is heaven (meaning, for example, eternal life in the presence of the creator), then practices such as prayer, fasting, vigils, and confession of sins may be in order to achieve healing. Other views of the problem and ultimate end entail emphasis on practices such as ethical behavior, moral purity, self-denial, ecstatic dance, trance, recitation of texts, incantations, or *mantras,* and so forth.

The Buddha's primary soteriological metaphor is that of the "path" (*magga*). This should be expected of a teacher who holds that the central problem of human existence is "pain" (*dukkha*), and that the ultimate goal of a human being is unbinding (*nibbāna/nirvāṇa*) from that pain. It should also be expected that practices directed to some external being or power are eschewed. Who or what receives a prayer? How? Through thought? We are reminded in this chapter that a thought, like every other "fabrication"—a visual object, a sound, a scent, a taste, and a tactile object—is nonsubstantial and impermanent. What force, then, could be inherent in the prayer? Where would it be located? To answer "God" to these questions, the Buddha claims, is really not to answer at all; it is, rather, to subscribe to a dogma. That is, it is to accept an answer based on others' opinions and views. Because no such claim or view is actually verifiable, such an "answer" is tantamount to belief in a rumor that one has heard.

In an image that is as humorous as it is disheartening, the Buddha said that this acceptance is like a group of blind people walking in single file. They walk on and on, "clinging to each other, and the first one sees nothing, the middle one sees nothing, and the last one sees nothing" (*Dīghanikāya* 13.15). So it is with those who look to gods or God for help. Although these traditions may have constructed elaborate theologies, institutions, rituals, and doctrines over the centuries that are "fully approved of, well transmitted, well cogitated, and well reflected on," the fact does not change the "empty, hollow, and false" nature of the claims (*Majjhimanikāya* 95.14).

In another image given by the Buddha, this elaborate construction of beliefs and claims is just like an ornate staircase built for a palace at a crossroads. But since *there is no actual palace there*, the staircase leads to empty space (*Dīghanikāya* 13.21). Any usage of theological language, which has embedded within it such far-ranging yet unprovable metaphysical presuppositions, is in the Buddha's view merely speculative. And speculative language is by nature "a thicket of views, a wilderness of views, a contortion of views, a vacillation of views, a fetter of views . . . beset by suffering, by vexation, by despair, and by fever, and does not lead to disenchantment, to dispassion, to cessation, to peace, to direct knowledge, to awakening, to unbinding" (*Majjhimanikāya* 72.14). It is precisely for this reason that the Buddha places a *path* where most traditions have a *view*.

For the Buddha, any solution to our human problem that is founded on a dogma about the state of things will fail. Whatever answer a person receives from others, and however fervently he or she may accept that answer, it does not change the fact that "there is birth, there is aging, there is death, there are sorrow, lamentation, pain, grief, and despair" (*Majjhimanikāya* 63.6). As a "physician," as opposed to a savior, the Buddha is concerned only to *show* the way to overcome the illness—the pain—of human existence. This is, in fact, one of the meanings of the Pāli term that is routinely translated as "teacher" in English: *desika*. A teacher is a teacher precisely by virtue of being adept at *pointing* at the matters of real and immediate concern, and *showing* the path to their resolution and fulfillment.

NOTES

273. *the eightfold.* This refers, of course, to the noble eightfold path. (See note 191.)

273. *the four statements.* The four noble truths. (See note 190.)

277. *fabrications.* "Fabrication" (*saṅkhāra*) is both a quality inherent in the process of perception (see note 62) and a quality of phenomenal objects (see note 203).

281. *three pathways of action.* That is, body, speech, and mind.

283. *craving-forests.* This is a playful verse. There is a wordplay on *vana*, which means both "woods" and "desire," and on *nibbanā*, "without craving," with its allusion to *nibbāna*, "unbinding." The manner in which these wordplays connect to each other is more obvious in Sanskrit, where the *v* is retained: *nirvana* < *nir* (without) + *vana* (desire): *nirvāṇa* (the *bb* cluster in the Pāli represents Sanskrit *rv*).

287. *intoxicated by possessions and children.* That is, being overly concerned with all of the "dust" that the householder's life entails.

CHAPTER TWENTY-ONE

SCATTERED THEMES
पकिण्णवग्गो

The verses in this chapter, as the title indicates, were apparently seen as lacking a unifying theme, hence, as being scattered, miscellaneous, or disjointed. But since the subjects of these verses have been met in various places in the *Dhammapada,* another way of understanding the title is as a reference to that very fact—that is, that the verses have been strewn throughout the work. The reader will quickly notice that the themes of the verses in this chapter have indeed been addressed in more detail elsewhere in the text: the importance of diligence, the dangers of anger, the power of mindfulness, the importance of gentleness, the value of renunciation and solitude, and the necessity of meditation. In this way, this chapter becomes a quick check against the reader's own possible creeping scatteredness!

NOTES

294–295. *the Brahmin goes undisturbed.* Because of their oblique language, these two verses may strike the reader as being out of place in the *Dhammapada.* This position assumes, of course, that the language means something other than what it says on the surface; namely, that Brahmins get away with murder. Is this a criticism of social privilege? Such social commentary is inconsistent with the rhetoric, imagery, and tenor of the rest of the text. So, should the verses be interpreted symbolically? This was the approach taken by the early commentarial tradition. In this understanding, the terms are to be equated as follows: mother = craving; father = conceit; the two warrior/ learned kings = the two extreme views of eternalism (perpetual life of the person as a stable identity or soul) and annihilationism (complete discontinuity of consciousness at death); kingdom = the twelve bases of consciousness (see note 146); retinue = pleasures dependent on the former; tiger = the hindrance of doubt; Brahmin = *arahant;* undisturbed = without suffering. (See John Ross Carter and Mahinda Palihawadana, *The Dhammapada* [Oxford: Oxford University Press, 1987], pp. 323–324.)

This approach makes good sense doctrinally, of course, but the equations are not nearly as clear as we normally find in the metaphors and similes of early Buddhist literature. As the reader will have noticed, the *Dhammapada* imagery is generally quite transparent. The symbolic correspondences given in the commentary, by contrast, are more reminiscent of the "twilight language" of medieval Vajrayāna Buddhism.

296. *Gotama.* The Buddha's birth name was Siddhattha Gotama (Sanskrit: Siddhārtha Gautama).

CHAPTER TWENTY-TWO

THE LOWER WORLD

निरयवग्गो

Buddhism holds that our cosmos is the place of *saṃsāra*, the ocean of be-coming. Impelled by the force of their intentional actions (*kamma/karma*), beings are caught in a whirlpool of recurring birth and death. The particular realm of rebirth depends on the nature of one's actions in the previous existence. (It is not the case, of course, that a "person" is reborn with prior identity intact but rather that that person's actions in the present life *condition* future "arisings" of that "stream" of consciousness. See the note to this introduction, and note 15–18.) The verses in this chapter refer to two types of birth/rebirth: "fortunate" and "unfortunate." Fortunate spheres of birth are the human world and certain "higher" planes, where radiant beings dwell. What makes these "fortunate" is that the beings in these realms possess a beneficial balance of pain and intelligence. The unfortunate places of rebirth are below there. (The Buddhists accepted the ancient Indian model of the universe as a three-tiered "triple world"; see note 30, "*radiant ones.*") These entail forms of being whereby pain and suffering predominate over intelligence. The lowest of these is called *niraya*. This term is typically translated as "hell." But since, unlike the Christian usage of the term, the Buddhists see this state as being as impermanent as any other form of existence, the term "hell" is unhelpful. If anything, *niraya* is closer to the concept of "purgatory," a place where negative fruits are borne and, hence, "purged." To avoid this misleading

Christian connotation, my translation of *niraya* as "lower world" sticks closely to the literal meaning of the term: to go down.

As the verses in this chapter make clear, falling to a lower form of existence is the result of one's own actions. There is no notion here of a supernatural being who judges those actions and condemns the person accordingly. Buddhists do, however, employ the Indian mythological figure Yama, the guardian of the underworld, to personalize this state of being. But as the following words of Yama clarify, the person who finds himself or herself in a "lower world" does not have to search far for the reason.

> Good [person], through negligence you have failed to do good by body, speech, and mind. Certainly they [the relatives and others who were affected by these actions] will deal with you according to your negligence. But this [detrimental] action of yours was not done by your mother or your father [or any of the others]; it was done by you yourself, and you yourself will experience the result.
>
> (*Majjhimanikāya* 3.4)

NOTES

Introduction to Chapter Twenty-two. One way to understand this notion of conditioning the stream of consciousness is to reflect on yourself as a six-year-old in relation to your present adult self. Is that child the same entity as you are now? Different? According to the Buddha, it is not correct to claim either "same" or "different." How can the two be the *same?* Physically, every molecule has turned over how many times? Mentally, you have developed a store of knowledge and increased your cognitive capacity a hundredfold. (We could name countless further aspects of the person to make this point; for example, evident changes in emotional life, speech patterns, talents, memory, preferences, and so on.) But neither is it quite accurate to say that you are *different* from that six-year-old. There is a discernible continuity between the two "moments" of your existence. This can be seen by looking closely at those same physical, mental, emotional, et cetera, qualities that have, paradoxically, changed in such obvious ways. So, in typical Buddhist parlance, it would be better to say that you are neither the same as *nor* different from that six-year-old. (Part of the problem rests with our usage of verbs of being. In what sense is an "entity" that is undergoing constant change and, hence, is insubstantial said to "be" at all? See also note 15–18.)

Readers wishing to explore this issue further are advised to begin with Steven Collins, *Selfless Persons: Imagery and Thought in Theravāda Buddhism* (Cambridge: Cambridge University Press, 1982), and Peter Harvey, *The Selfless Mind: Personality and Consciousness, and Nirvana in Early Buddhism* (Surrey: Curzon Press, 1995).

307. *wear the yellow.* A reference to the monk's robe.

ELEPHANT

नागवग्गो

The elephant has played an important role in Indian civilization since more than a thousand years before the birth of the Buddha. There is evidence to suggest that in the great Indus Valley cities of Harrapā and Mohenjo-Daro (ca. 2000 B.C.E.) the elephant was trained to perform tasks associated with building construction. By the time of the Buddha, the elephant had become an elite fighting animal. Its massive body arrayed with thick leather armor, with shimmering metal spikes on its tusks and swords mounted on its trunk, carrying two or three soldiers, each armed with spears, bows and arrows, maces, and javelins, the elephant was, as one scholar has put it, "rather like tanks in modern warfare, breaking up the enemy's ranks and smashing palisades, gates, and other defenses." Given their capacity in warfare, ownership of elephants was limited to kings and ruling chieftains. In this way, the elephant began to take on the aura of royalty.

This battle rhetoric may appear unseemly in a Buddhist text. But in this chapter the elephant is presented as an exemplar of the advancing practitioner. Time is running short; the *Dhammapada* is nearly complete. The ideal reader should be approaching the insight and understanding that will carry him or her through to the end. Now, the text seems to be indicating, strength and power are required to win the battle. The battle to be won, of course, is not against some external enemy but against oneself. Like an elephant bearing arrows in battle, the practitioner must become capable of enduring insults slung by others.

Endurance for elephants, as for Buddhists, is not the mournful and passive acceptance of harsh circumstances. Only a well-trained elephant can restrain itself enough to endure battle wounds without going mad with fear and anger. So, for endurance to be beneficial and productive in the life of a practitioner, it must be coupled with genuine progress in the mastery of verbal, physical, and mental restraint. In the Buddhist view expressed here, strength and restraint follow from the practitioner's skillful ability to watch his or her mind. And when this is done with diligence and delight, the advanced practitioner is able to pull himself out of any onslaught of misfortune or insult "like an elephant, sunk in mud."

NOTES

Introduction to Chapter Twenty-three. *"like tanks in modern warfare."* See A. L. Basham, *The Wonder That Was India* (New York: Grove Press, 1954), p. 129.

323. *unreached realm.* A synonym for *nibbāna/nirvāṇa*.

CHAPTER TWENTY-FOUR

CRAVING

तण्हावग्गो

Maybe, after all of what has preceded, we might understand something of craving. Not that the preceding was necessary for such an understanding, since craving accompanies us everywhere, every moment of our lives. Craving stands, too, at the beginning of the Buddha's teaching, as the second noble truth, which identifies it as the immediate cause of pain. But in being placed near the very end of the text, this chapter on craving has a special poignancy. Before, the human proclivity to craving and grasping may have seemed as natural as our compulsion to eat and sleep. Now, having contemplated the many assertions, claims, exhortations, practical exercises, warnings, and insights and observations of human conduct offered through the verses of the *Dhammapada,* the reader may indeed finally see craving for what it is: a creeping vine. Creeping vines entangle, ensnare, and strangle the life out of that to which they have attached themselves. Maybe by now the reader has developed some aspiration to ease up on incessant plunging after objects of desire, "like a monkey seeking fruit in the forest." Maybe the reader will not reject so quickly the image of himself or herself as scurrying about, "harassed by craving," like a hare being hunted in the woods.

At this late moment, a voice appears in the first person, as if the Buddha is speaking to us bluntly and directly:

> I speak to you this auspicious word,
> to all of you assembled here.

Maybe now this word will be received as it is intended—as indeed every word of every verse of the *Dhammapada* has been intended— namely, as a compelling exhortation directed to a real person leading a real life. The blunt language of these verses is the best evidence that this chapter is meant to convey a sense of urgency. But like the stark imagery, it is not without promise and hope.

NOTES

339. *thirty-six streams.* Although the verses of this chapter are beneficially read with a commonsensical understanding of craving, this verse refers to a more technical meaning. In "The Discourse Setting in Motion the Wheel of the Doctrine" (*Dhammacakkappavattana Sutta*), the professed first teaching of the recently awakened Buddha, craving is defined as that "which leads to re-newed existence, accompanied by delight and lust, seeking delight here and there; that is, craving for sensual pleasures, craving for existence, craving for extermination" (see *Saṃyuttanikāya* 5.56.11). The "thirty-six streams" are these three modes of craving multiplied by the six internal bases of con-sciousness plus the six external bases of consciousness—all of which "flow mightily toward what is pleasing": $3(6+6)=36$. (See note 146.)

350. *meditates on the unpleasant.* Reference to a practical exercise meant to reduce attraction to physical objects. (See note 8.)

351. *final embodiment.* A reference to the *arahant*.

CHAPTER TWENTY-FIVE

THE PRACTITIONER

भिक्खुवग्गो

Like that of the previous two chapters, the tone of this chapter is finality and decisiveness. The verses here presume that through application of thoughtful reading, the lessons have been learned, and through application of the prescribed practices of mindfulness and meditation, some measure of direct insight has been realized. Each of the themes treated in this chapter—restraint, meditation, mindfulness, and the fruit of these, ease—has been met before in the text. What is different here is the way they are presented, namely, as final instructions on the way. They have the tone of a casting off: you have been taught, instructed, provided with reasons, even warned; now go, and do what has to be done!

The "author" of these verses visualizes a reader whose countenance has been deeply transformed through serious engagement with the text. Because that person has acquired the skill of living with body, voice, and mind restrained, his or her face reveals that he or she possesses "inner delight, [is] composed, solitary, and content." Imagine the face of a person who, trusting in the teachings of the Buddha as encountered in the text, has actually *arrived* at the empty, peaceful place, where fabrication is stilled and pain has ceased. What would your face look like, so filled with extraordinary delight? What would your face look like with your mind at peace?

> For those who understand,
> this is the deathless.

It is *that* one who is called "practitioner."

NOTES

361. *practitioner.* The word that I am translating in the title and throughout this chapter as "practitioner" is *bhikkhu.* This is the Buddha's term for those who wandered around India begging alms as a means of sustaining themselves on the path. It is almost unanimously translated as "monk." As used by the Buddha, however, this is an anachronism. The order (*saṅgha*) founded by the Buddha was composed of itinerant practitioners. While there is evidence that these mendicants would settle into community living during the rainy season, the picture that emerges is not yet that of a "monastery," if by that term we mean an institution roughly comparable to the permanently sedentary life of a medieval European cloister. So, since there were no monasteries in the Buddha's day, there were no monks.

Even after the establishment of settled communities, the terms *bhikkhu* and *bhikkhunī* (the feminine form) retained their reference to the practice of itinerant alms begging. The terms are derived from the desiderative form ("desiring to do X," "wishing for X") of the verbal root *bhaj.* This verb is rich in meaning and significance for Indian religions. Its basic sense is "to divide, distribute, share with"; but already in the Mahābhārata, the great epic of the fourth century B.C.E., it has the meaning "to practice, pursue, cultivate." Its best known derivative is *bhakti,* "to worship, to practice devotion," presumably from the fact that Hindu worshipers offer—share—food, water, incense, music, and praise to visual icons of the venerated deity. So, all of this, coupled with my interest in making the *Dhammapada* more accessible to the modern reader, has informed the translation of *bhikkhu* as "practitioner." (On Buddhist monasticism, see Mohan Wijayaratna, *Buddhist Monastic Life: According to the Texts of the Theravāda Tradition* [Cambridge: Cambridge University Press, 1990].)

368. *Dwelling in loving kindness.* This refers to cultivation of one of the four qualities known as the "sublime abidings" (*brahmavihāras*). The four traits are loving kindness, compassion, sympathetic joy, and equanimity. The verse may also refer to a meditative practice whereby the practitioner "suffuses" the world with feelings of loving kindness.

> Then, with his heart filled with loving-kindness, [the practitioner] dwells suffusing one quarter, the second, the third, the fourth. Thus he dwells

suffusing the whole world, upwards, downwards, across, everywhere, always with a heart filled with loving-kindness, abundant, unbounded, without hate or ill-will. (*Dīghanikāya* 13.78)

The *brahmavihāras* are known as the "four immeasurables" because of this "abundant, unbounded" scope of their application. In the meditation exercise, the practitioner should leave "nothing untouched, nothing unaffected in the sensuous sphere" (*kāmadhātu;* see note 30, *"radiant ones"; Dīghanikāya* 79). Loving kindness (*mettāvihāra*) is also considered a particularly effective antidote to the powerful human tendency toward aggression and violence.

370. *Five attachments.* The five traits to be cut off are the lower or coarse fetters (see notes 31, *"every fetter,"* and 218, *"one who is streaming upward"*); the five to be abandoned are the higher or subtle fetters; the five to be further cultivated are the faculties of faith, energy, mindfulness, concentration, and insight or wisdom; and the five attachments are passion, aversion, delusion, self-importance, and wrong views.

373–374. *the empty place... the deathless.* Synonyms for *nibbāna/nirvāṇa.*

375. *the discipline.* This refers to the disciplinary regulations codified in the section of the *Vinaya* known as the *Pātimokkha,* or "that which is binding" to the *bhikkhus* and *bhikkhunīs.*

CHAPTER TWENTY-SIX

THE SUPERIOR PERSON

ब्राह्मणवग्गो

In his boldest act of linguistic inversion, the Buddha calls that person a Brahmin—a superior person—who contradicts, in every detail, everything that he held an actual Brahmin to be. Brahmins (*brāhmaṇa*, the word in the chapter title) were the self-proclaimed superiors of Indian society. They took their name from the fact that they alone had the knowledge to control the *brahman*, the potency inherent in the words uttered in the Vedic sacrificial rituals. These rituals were necessary to propitiate the resplendent powers (*deva*) of earth, sky, and heaven to grant the propitiators health and abundance, and to uphold the cosmic order. But to the Buddha, the Brahmins' knowledge of the *devas* and the powers of coercion that that knowledge entailed were nothing more than a manipulative display of self-delusion. In the end, the Buddha bluntly stated, "the talk of these Brahmins learned in the three Vedas turns out to be laughable, mere words, empty, and vain" (*Dīghanikāya* 13.15).

> Those Brahmins learned in the three Vedas who persistently neglect what a Brahmin should do, declare: "We call on Indra, Soma, Varuṇa, Isāna, Pajāpati, Brahmā, Mahiddhi, Yama." But that such Brahmins . . . will, as a consequence of their calling, begging, requesting, or wheedling, attain after death, at the breaking up of the body, to union with Brahmā (God)—that is just not possible. (*Dīghanikāya* 13.25)

It is not difficult to accept this statement as a critique of privileged religious officials both then and now—officials, moreover, who fall far short of the ideals they interminably preach to others. But can it be understood in a way that is more directly relevant to the reader? What is it that *the reader* "should do" in order to fulfill his or her promise as a superior member of society? Such a person, in giving up all expectations, becomes as "clear and pure as the moon,/luminous, serene." But the way to this clarity and brilliance is through the "difficult, muddy path," through "the bewilderment that is the swirl of becoming." Is it a paradox that clear understanding is born in bewilderment, in the very mire of the mind?

The final verses of the *Dhammapada* tell us that the traveler has "crossed over, reached the other shore," become "free from desire, free from doubt, not grasping," perfected in knowledge, awakened, unbound.

Is that really possible?

NOTES

383. *modes of fabrication.* See notes 62 and 203.

383. *the uncreated.* A synonym for *nibbāna/nirvāṇa.*

384. *twofold practice.* Presumably the two aspects of meditation: calming (*samatha*) and insight (*vipassanā*) (*Dīghanikāya* 33.1.9 [23]). Calming practices, such as mindfulness centered on breathing (*ānāpānasati*), achieve the concentrated attentiveness (*samādhi*) necessary for "wisdom" (*paññā*), that is, a direct insight into the nature of mind and phenomena. (See notes 27 and 144.)

388. *"seeker."* For the wordplay on "seeker," see note 265.

388. *Sending forth toxins . . . "one who has gone forth."* A play on words. A person is "one who has gone forth" (*pabbajita*), i.e., become a Buddhist mendicant, by virtue of having "sent forth" (*pabbājaya*) toxins from his mind.

392. *as a Brahmin honors the sacrificial fire.* A reference to the *yajña*, the ritual mentioned in the chapter introduction. Here, "Brahmin" refers, of course, to the caste, whose members are "superior" by "means of ancestry" only, as the following verse indicates.

393–394. *matted hair . . . deerskin clothing.* References to asceticism. In their extreme form—as radical austerity and bodily mortification—the Buddha rejected such practices as useless, indeed harmful, to the actualization of the path. He favored such practices, however, in their moderate form, as, for example, exercises of self-restraint.

The following statement by the Buddha clarifies his position on this matter of extreme importance to the *samaṇa* traditions of his day. (The present reader, too, should see this as a relevant issue in the practice of Buddhism in the modern West.) This passage is also interesting for the images of ancient ascetic practice conveyed. As the reader will notice, the Buddha equates "ascetic" with "Brahmin" here, but only after redefining both terms to correspond to what he considers the vital and indispensable matters of religious practice. (I have abbreviated the passage without ellipses for ease of reading.)

A man becomes a herb-eater, a millet-eater, an eater of grass, cow dung, of forest roots and fruits. He wears coarse hemp or mixed material, shrouds from corpses, rags from the dust heap, bark shavings, horse hair. He is a plucker-out of hair and beard, devoted to this practice, he is a covered-thorn man, making his bed on them, sleeping alone in a garment of wet mud, living in the open air, living on filth and addicted to the practice, or he dwells intent on the practice of going to bathe three times before evening.

A practicer of self-mortification may do all of these things, but if his morality, his heart and his wisdom are not developed and brought to realization, then indeed he is still far from being an ascetic or a Brahmin. But, when a monk [*bhikkhu* > practitioner] develops non-enmity, non-ill-will and a heart full of loving kindness and, abandoning the impulses, realizes and dwells in the uncorrupted deliverance of mind, the deliverance through wisdom, having realized it in this very life by his own insight, then that [practitioner] is termed an ascetic and a Brahmin. (*Dīghanikāya* 8.15)

Acknowledgments

Charles Hallisey taught me how to read. I hope that what I have written in this book reflects a little of what I have learned from him. I am grateful to Kai Riedl, friend and ideal reader, who patiently worked through the entire text, making many thoughtful suggestions for improvement. He has made this a more honest book. I am thankful to Will Murphy of Random House for his willingness to take on this project, and for the concern that he has shown it from the very outset. Ulrich Baer has given me help and support in many ways through the years, and I am grateful to him for that. I cannot begin to express the appreciation that I feel for my wife, Friederike, and daughters, Alexandra and Mia. Because of the way that they are, and the lives that we lead together, I am able to spend time—often with them—exploring the teachings of the Buddha. I was fortunate to have had such good friends when I was first making sense of all of this, long ago. Thank you, Thom Adams, Cordy Swope, Paul Della Pelle, Rich Hutchins, Damon Wallis, Franklin Anderson, Peter Ritchie, and Douglas Wolff. (They are the moss among the ruins.) To Bruce, my teacher of long ago, whose last name I no longer know, I offer my gratitude for introducing me to the *Dhammapada*. Who could have known the fruits of those seeds?

ABOUT THE TRANSLATOR

GLENN WALLIS has a Ph.D. in Sanskrit and Indian Studies from Harvard and is assistant professor of religion at the University of Georgia. He is the author of numerous articles on Buddhism and *Mediating the Power of Buddhas*.

A Note on the Type

The principal text of this Modern Library edition
was set in a digitized version of Janson, a typeface that
dates from about 1690 and was cut by Nicholas Kis,
a Hungarian working in Amsterdam. The original matrices have
survived and are held by the Stempel foundry in Germany.
Hermann Zapf redesigned some of the weights and sizes for
Stempel, basing his revisions on the original design.